P9-DWT-059

THE FOLLOW-THROUGH FACTOR

GENE C. HAYDEN·

THE
FOLLOW-
THROUGH
FACTOR

GETTING FROM DOUBT TO DONE

McClelland & Stewart

Library and Archives Canada Cataloguing in Publication

Hayden, Gene C.
   The follow-through factor : getting from doubt to done / Gene C. Hayden.

ISBN 978-0-7710-3818-1

  1. Goal (Psychology). 2. Achievement motivation.
3. Persistence. 4. Success – Psychological aspects. I. Title.

BF505.G6H38 2009   158.1   C2009-903892-7

We acknowledge the financial support of the Government of Canada through the Book Publishing Industry Development Program and that of the Government of Ontario through the Ontario Media Development Corporation's Ontario Book Initiative. We further acknowledge the support of the Canada Council for the Arts and the Ontario Arts Council for our publishing program.

Published simultaneously in the United States of America by McClelland & Stewart Ltd., P.O. Box 1030, Plattsburgh, New York 12901

Library of Congress Control Number: 2009934802

Typeset in Sabon by M&S, Toronto
Printed and bound in Canada

ANCIENT FOREST
FRIENDLY

This book was produced using ancient-forest friendly papers.

McClelland & Stewart Ltd.
75 Sherbourne Street
Toronto, Ontario
M5A 2P9
www.mcclelland.com

1 2 3 4 5   14 13 12 11 10

— CONTENTS —

Once upon a time, I would have said that I was the last person in the world who should write a book on follow-through. I wasn't particularly adept at sticking with my goals. Of course, I had my reasons.

Not long after I began working as a business reporter, I decided my true calling was to be a playwright. To make the transition, I figured I would go back to school and get a master's degree in drama. But I dropped that idea when I learned I would need three undergraduate courses in theatre before I could qualify for the program. That seemed like a lot of work just to get to the starting gate.

Instead, I resolved to become a full-time travel writer after assignments to write about Australia and Florida fell into my lap. But oddly enough, invitations to cover exotic places didn't keep raining from the sky. If I was to make the rent every month, I was going to have to start pitching story ideas to travel editors. At the time, the ratio of rejection to success for a fledgling travel writer was 25 to 1. Why put myself through that?

Truthfully, I just wanted to write fiction anyway. After fifteen years as a journalist, I became a partner in a PR agency. While at the agency, I wrote just enough of a manuscript to get accepted into prestigious creative writing programs, twice. I cringe even now to admit that I dropped out, both times. But I just didn't have the time to produce new copy every week.

Shamefully, I could go on and on. My career as a humour columnist had just picked up steam when I got cold feet, worried that maybe people would start to think I really wasn't very funny after all.

Some people are born terriers. When they get hold of a bone, they don't drop it for anything. That would not have been me. For more damning evidence, take a tour of my basement. Under cobwebs, you will find an unused elliptical machine and weights, a digital piano with the beginner's instruction guide still in plastic, a never-assembled easel, and a file cabinet stuffed with incomplete grant applications, half-written manuscripts, unopened teach-yourself-Italian CDS, and home-exchange catalogues with their spines intact.

In my defence, I came naturally by my habit of never doing anything more than flirting with an idea. I spent most of my childhood in a car, driving the highways of Europe with my mother, who chased dreams, never catching them. With my sister in the passenger seat and me in the back, we criss-crossed Europe so many times that countries, cities, and schools all blurred together like the design on a spinning top.

I can't remember many details of my youth, but I can recall my mother's tales of what she would accomplish when we hit the next town. She would open a language school, start a travel club, work as a multilingual interpreter, launch a newspaper for expats, set up a theatre company. Smart, resourceful, beautiful, fluent in four languages – I truly thought she could do whatever she wanted.

I had reason to believe. Wherever we went, my mother always landed jobs, even though she didn't have the necessary work permits. She found furnished apartments to rent despite being unable to pay the required last-month deposit or provide references. She managed to talk reluctant school principals into letting us attend our age grades at public schools, even when we didn't speak the local language.

Each time we drove into a new town, I was certain we had found the place where my mother's idea would take root and change our lives. And when two, three, or six months later we were back on the road, I believed my mother when she explained that the circumstances had not been right. My older sister would look back at me from the front seat and roll her eyes, but she found no ally in me. My sister didn't understand what my mother was up against, but I did. It wasn't my mother's fault if there wasn't a demand for English lessons in Stitches, Spain. She couldn't have known that she would be unable to meet the right person to introduce her to the expat community in Athens.

When I was thirteen, my sister returned to our hometown of Montreal to attend university and I moved up to the front seat. My perspective changed when I became the one to spend hour after hour staring straight ahead. I started to notice how so many long stretches of road are interchangeable. Simultaneously, I became aware of how my mother's many stories of what she would and could do, if only, were equally repetitive. But I had to make a choice. I could decide that no matter how brilliant my mother's ideas were, they would never be anything more than tumbleweeds blowing in the wind because she was unable, or unwilling, to figure out how to pin one down. Or I could continue to believe that she was simply a victim of circumstances and that eventually we would stumble onto perfect conditions that would allow her to fulfill her goals.

Life on the road is often excruciatingly lonely. Rather than distance myself from my only companion, I opted to join her in decrying the regrettable obstacles that prevented her from achieving her plans. And to keep reading maps to help her find her Emerald City.

Eventually it was my time to vacate the front seat and return to Canada. I took a flight from Nice to Montreal. From the plane window, I gave my mother the fingers-crossed sign while I watched her pull out of the airport parking lot and make a right to Italy. She never stopped chasing rainbows.

Twenty-seven years after I boarded that plane, she died at eighty-four, with a ticket to Sydney, Australia, in her purse and a plan to start a network for single travellers while there.

As for me, I went into journalism to have a profession that would enable me to continue to do what I knew best – roam. I spent years globe-trotting and interviewing people from all walks of life who had achieved their ambitions. To be honest, these people irked me, quite a bit. Why did fortune smile on them and not my mother? What did they have that she didn't?

While in my early twenties, I decided the high-flyers must have special, unique qualities that set them apart from the rest of us mere mortals. But it didn't take long for the stars to fall from my eyes. I quickly began to recognize that many I spoke with weren't super brilliant, extraordinarily creative, wildly daring, or drop-dead gorgeous. They'd be the first to admit that they never tipped any scale when it came to talent, brains, beauty, or creativity. So, I wondered, what separated them from others who had equal potential but nothing to show for it but frustration?

Of course, some people do have a leg up over others. I interviewed a fair number who truly had a competitive advantage. These were the born artists and visionaries, the natural athletes, and the people with family names that opened doors. But of the many hundreds I talked to over my career, these genetic lottery winners were in the minority. Most were just average folk, coping with the same doubts and struggles as the next person.

5

I grew increasingly obsessed with figuring out why some people pursued their goals while so many others, with equivalent talents and desires, just kept driving round and round on highways, getting nowhere.

Over the years, I devoured countless motivational books and attended umpteen big-ticket inspirational lectures and seminars worldwide to research what the experts had to say on the subject. To sum up their advice, they said the secret to success was faith, commitment, focus, courage, passion, and determination. If you didn't know better, you'd think you had to be a superhero in a red cape and spandex tights to take on a new project or start a new business. But I knew that wasn't the case for the many hundreds of goal-getters I met.

For the first half of my career, I hopscotched from one job to another. I didn't jump quite as fast as my mother changed cities, but I had learned restlessness from her. For once, it served me well. I was the "People" editor of Canada's national newsweekly magazine for several years, and before that an editor with the country's national music magazine. As well, for more than a decade, I worked for an assortment of business and other publications in North America and Europe. This string of jobs allowed me up-close access to a large and diverse number of people who had triumphed, failed, and triumphed again at challenges of every conceivable nature.

Relentlessly, I questioned all those I interviewed to determine how they differed from my parent, colleague, or

6

neighbour, or myself. And on almost every occasion, I found they were more similar than not. Many who had attained their goals admitted to me that they weren't always madly, passionately in love with their current project. I also heard from people who pursued their ambition without being swim-with-the-sharks gutsy. I talked with hundreds who managed to climb their personal mountains despite being plagued with fears and self-doubt, and just as many who said that they weren't by nature energetic, intuitive, or single-mindedly focused. "Listen," confessed a successful theatre director, "I don't want people knowing this, but beneath this hundred-dollar haircut you'll find the brain of a nervous nebbish. And yet I managed to start a theatre company. Go figure."

I continued to investigate the differences between people who were all talk and those who were all action, after I made yet another career move, this time to join a public relations firm that turned products into household names and people into media and corporate stars. I had transitioned from chronicling people's success to helping make it happen. I was now in the business of handholding, walking clients step by step through strategies to position themselves and their products as leaders in their field. And in becoming an operator of the dream machine, I was able to put together the last pieces of a puzzle that I had brooded over for ages.

The follow-through factor

When I had the answer to how to achieve your goals despite everything and anything, I wanted very much to return to the passenger seat of the car in which I had grown up to share what I knew. But I was too late. So instead, I became a certified coach.

I help clients clarify their aspirations and figure out practical strategies for winning the tug-of-war against circumstances and doubts that hold them back from reaching their goals. By the time I started to write this book, I had worked with thousands, individually, in corporate teams, at workshops and conferences. Over years of listening to people of all ages and from all backgrounds detail their ambitions, I discovered that ultimately we all seek the same thing: momentum.

Individuals have their specific goals, but the overarching desire to experience forward movement is universal. Simply put, standing still eventually becomes tedious, on both a personal and professional level. And worse, we are beset by the uneasy sense that while others may be creating interesting stories full of twists and turns for their lives, we don't have a narrative that excites us.

A lot of people stand still – or travel in circles, which amounts to the same thing – not because they enjoy it, but because they are unsure how to get around the very real obstacles that litter the way to achieving a goal. When I hold workshops, I often open by asking participants if they have

8

ever had valid reasons for giving up on pursuing an ambition. It never fails that all heads nod.

Inevitably, there are overwhelming obstacles that get between us and our great idea. And it's entirely understandable that when we hit a particularly daunting barricade we retreat in defeat to our original position. But those who manage to successfully reach their goal don't withdraw. Instead, they problem-solve their way around every brick wall they encounter. And yet I can confirm from years of research that most people who push through don't have any more confidence, money, know-how, or time than anyone else. So how do they do it? They have something I call the *follow-through factor*. This factor is the only thing that separates the doers from the dreamers.

The follow-through factor is a deal you make with yourself to fulfill a personal interest or goal. It's an iron-clad promise to oneself that you will do whatever it takes to experience that which is important to you. Those with the follow-through factor say it is this handshake that drives them to persevere with their ambitions even when life isn't making it easy.

There is no turning back when you make a deal. You feel duty bound to somehow tackle all the hurdles that stand in your way. Of course, you can renege on the contract with yourself and allow circumstances to determine your life, but you pay a price in disappointment and frustration. At that point, holding to your bargain is the more painless option,

9

regardless of the hassles and headaches that you may have to overcome to do so. In my case, it would have been less heartbreaking to cram some theatre courses into an already busy schedule, pitch travel ideas and suffer some rejection, or limp to the finish of a creative writing program than to let myself down – over and over again.

Those who have the follow-through factor run the very same obstacle course to reach their desired destination that everyone does. The difference is they don't accept that any problem is greater than the pact they made with themselves. And anyone can acquire the follow-through factor. It's a matter of honouring the deal between who you are and who you want to be.

How to use this book

In these pages, you'll discover the way of thinking of people who have made a personal vow to pursue their ambitions, against the odds. You'll hear what they say to themselves to keep going when they're faced with the very real dilemmas and doubts that commonly stop so many of us from following through on our goals. You'll learn practical, tried-and-proven strategies and exercises to develop and strengthen your own deal with yourself.

The road to good intentions is littered with the word "but." How many of us have said, I do want to follow through but . . . I don't have the time, the money, the energy, the know-how, the patience, the guts, the passion, the help, the confidence, etc.? Every chapter in this book tackles a "but" that is known to block the road to achievement. You'll find out what people who have the follow-through factor do to push past that particular obstacle.

Your obstacles will change as you progress in following through on your ambition. You may be moving along at a good clip after having adopted strategies to conquer your impatience, only to turn a corner and come face to face with fear of failure. Pick and choose the chapters and exercises as they apply to you at different stages in your journey. But make a point of starting by reading the first four chapters, which are dedicated to explaining the follow-through factor and helping you determine whether your idea is right for you. Each chapter in the book ends with a follow-through factor cue card, a quick reminder of the tactics achievers rely on to prevent themselves from backtracking on their path.

Peppered throughout the book are "notes to self." These are helpful tips for dealing with the vocal critics on the sidelines who will insist, for your own good, that you turn around and run when you encounter an obstruction on your journey. You'll recognize skeptical friends, naysayer relatives, or cynical colleagues among those who will tell you to be realistic, sensible, and safe. But the loudest voice of rebuke may be that of your own inner critic. Think of "notes to self" as your mute button for negativity.

The follow-through factor works. It has the power to take you from doubt to done. I have proof. I have seen hundreds of clients apply the ideas and strategies detailed in this book to move from uncertainty and wistfulness to accomplishment. And like my clients, I too have learned to stop relegating my personal interests and aspirations to my basement.

Would the follow-through factor have brought the spinning top that was my life with my mother to a stop? I am convinced it would have. An ambition is only as good as the promise you make to it. It would have saved us a lot of disappointment, and gas money, if we had known then that it was not the obstacles that stopped my mother from fulfilling her ambitions, it was her absence of a promise to do so.

My hope is that you make a deal to follow through in turning your ideas and aspirations into reality. As soon as you do, you will find yourself moving forward, all the while creating colourful stories that will be meaningful to you. There's no but about it.

ONE

Yes, but what is follow-through?

Follow-through is a choice, disguised as a major headache and potential time-waster. As an option, it doesn't sell itself well. If you go with it, you put faith and effort on the line. If you choose not to exercise it, nobody cares. People aren't even going to notice. You can be fairly sure that no one will signal "loser alert" behind your back when you enter a room. Of course, no one will be jumping up to pat you on the back either, but you'll still likely get asked to meetings and dinners on occasion.

That's the tragedy of the matter. The worst thing that happens to those of us who fall short in follow-through is nothing. Life goes on as is. Nothing happens. Just as the opposite of love isn't hate but indifference, the opposite of success isn't failure, it's status quo. And that's fine. Except that for the ambitious among us, *fine* is a four-letter word.

And I'll tell you what else is all too fine. Most of us feel we've got plenty of follow-through. So when we're frustrated

13

that we're not where we want to be, we don't accept that our problem might be neatly summed up in one hyphenated word: follow-through. As we tick off all the reasons why we aren't achieving our goals, it never even dawns on us to include follow-through on our list And why would it? We get our assignments done. We meet our targets. We get our reports completed, our vacations planned, our closets sorted. Perhaps that last one is going a bit too far, but many of us have, at one point in our history, assembled an apartment's worth of IKEA furniture, and what better proof of our determination and grit could there be than that?

Just as we all think we're better drivers than we are (truthfully, do you stop the recommended three seconds at *every* stop sign?), most of us of tend to think we're stronger at follow-through than we are. That's because we typically misinterpret follow-through as being something different than it is. Contrary to popular belief, follow-through is not the same as commitment. In fact, compared to follow-through, commitment is a walk in the park.

Commitment vs. follow-through

Slide commitment and follow-through under a microscope and you'll detect a key difference. Commitment is discipline; follow-through is a state of mind. Commitment comes with a how-to manual. If you want to build a cabinet, read the diagram. If you want to lose weight, stick to a diet and exercise program. If you want to climb a mountain, complete a training program. If you want to buy a house, adhere to a savings plan. If you want to write a book, hold fast to a writing schedule. Commitment demands double-fisted resolve but delivers a predictable return on effort. You know what you'll end up with if you commit to your plan.

Commitment is a map with well-marked roads that you can travel to arrive at your destination, whereas follow-through is more of a pirate's treasure map. You have to figure out for yourself how to get to the X between the palm trees. You are inevitably going to have to problem-solve as you make your way through uncharted territory, with little more than a vague sense of which direction you should head first. Venturing into the unknown requires an adventurous mind, since you can never be sure what awaits you around the next corner or how you are going to tackle the unexpected. You may arrive at your Emerald City quickly, or you may take longer than expected and encounter more obstructions than you could have anticipated. But follow-through offers this guarantee to the wary: if you persist, you'll get to some place you want to be and you'll arrive much wiser.

Follow-through and commitment work in tandem. Commitment is the body of your idea, follow-through is its legs.

Say you decide to write a book on the elves of Iceland. You need commitment to churn out three hundred pages about Iceland's invisible population. If you stick firmly to your research and writing schedule, you can guarantee that your investment of hard work will result in a manuscript. But once you have printed out three hundred pages, you are faced with the daunting question "Now what?" Having a manuscript in a drawer won't change your life, it won't make you a published author, it won't broadcast to the world that you're an expert on Icelandic beliefs. If you just leave your manuscript in the drawer, all you will have is three hundred pages that'll gather dust over time.

The only way to bind those pages into a book with your name on the spine is to flex your follow-through. And that means taking a deep breath and putting time, money, and, toughest of all, ego on the line to send that book to every agent and, perhaps after that, every publisher in the English-speaking world. You can't know what the result of your efforts will be, which is extremely nerve-wracking. If you think writing a book is tough, sending it out for possible rejection by every single person in the book publishing world is like going through root canals, tooth after tooth.

Follow-through is the *only* thing that separates the dreamers from the goal-getters. If you get nothing but rejection slips in the mail, it's follow-through again that will keep you going and trying something else you have no experience with – self-publishing. If that's the road you take, you'll need to venture further into uncharted territory to figure out how to promote and distribute your self-published book. Certainly, in the end, it's only because you exercised follow-through that you'll be able to call yourself a published author, highlight the fact on your resumé, and introduce yourself forever more by saying, "You may have seen my book."

Best-case scenario: Getting your manuscript published, or self-publishing, will launch your career as an author. Worst-case scenario: You can mention your book to distinguish yourself from the competition when you meet a potential client or employer or a blind date. In either case, following through will have created new possibilities for you. And you'll feel better about yourself than if you had just put your untouched manuscript in a box in your basement.

Think of follow-through as a free fall compared to commitment's bungee jump. Sure, to bungee jump you need to psych yourself up and find the guts to leap off the edge. But let's not forget, you're going off the bridge with a harness secured to your waist. You can plot out in advance how the jump will proceed and how many times you'll swing back and forth before you are pulled back on the bridge. With follow-through, you jump out of a plane with your eye on a designated landing spot, but for all you know a sudden gust of wind could blow you off track and leave you dangling on a farmer's backyard laundry line, miles from your target. As a result, you may have to figure out how to detangle yourself and either hike a few unexpected miles or sweet-talk your way into getting a tractor ride.

Typical to follow-through, you can never be sure how the path will unfold, which is why it requires a leap of faith. And as the following chapters show, such faith may often be

17

tested, in different ways. But those with the follow-through factor have strategies to share for winning every test, and illuminating perspectives to guide you on your path. As you set off, here's one piece of good news. You no longer have to count on luck to help you.

Follow-through doesn't require luck (although a little luck never hurt anyone)

Playwright Tennessee Williams said, "Luck is believing you're lucky." When you think you've got chance on your side, you allow yourself to take risks. And eventually, one risk or another pays off. It's a numbers game. You can pay thousands of dollars to attend a conference on the other side of the country and still not meet an interesting contact or a potential spouse there. But the more events you attend, the more you expand your network. When you finally encounter the person who helps you attain your goal, it wasn't luck that played matchmaker, it was the series of risks that you took.

My client Adam didn't define luck as risk-taking; he thought it was more like finding the perfect parking spot on a busy shopping street, something that happens through no doing of your own. And he believed it was what you needed to succeed. So when Adam couldn't grow his accounting business despite being committed and adept, he figured his problem was simply "bad luck." He explained that while his current clients were loyal enough, they weren't giving him additional work or many referrals. He concluded that they weren't the sort of people who liked to pass around business cards. And those who had extra work that he could handle had already hired others to do it.

"I have a real talent for what I do," Adam said in our first meeting. "I do my job exceptionally well, and my rates are very competitive. So you'd think the phone would ring off the hook. But it doesn't."

"What's your follow-through plan?" I asked.

"I'm following through by committing to doing a great job in the first place. One great job should lead to another. I've proved myself, I've proved my talent; that should be good enough," said Adam.

"Yet, sad to say, there're a lot of really talented people out there flipping burgers," I noted.

Adam shrugged. "Well, a lot of talented people aren't lucky."

Or they don't think they are.

In Adam's case, he was uncomfortable asking his clients for more business or referrals. He was desperate to increase his income, and was terrified that he might let his neediness show. So he convinced himself that if he just focused on doing good work, business would improve on its own. Basically, his approach was to leave his destiny to the whims of fate. That's not follow-through; that's finger-crossing.

So often we feel that if we do a job well, the reward will follow of its own accord. If only life were like that. If it were, everyone with a great website would be fabulously wealthy. So many people I've interviewed have dedicated enormous amounts of time to working on a knock-your-socks-off website or Web feature to drive their business. They've spent months revising copy, worrying over graphics and drop-down menus, and plotting navigation paths. You could renovate a three-storey house in the time they took to finish their site. And when they're finally done, they fall into a bad case of the post-website blues, because their website is now all dressed up, but no one's noticing.

Sometimes we are our own worst enemies. We all want to believe the famous line from the movie *Field of Dreams*, "If you build it, they will come." It's a nice idea that sounds wise, but it really isn't much of a business plan. Still, we buy in, so when people don't come after we've built it, we shrug dejectedly and tell ourselves that it must be because they found someplace better to go. We feel as if everyone is having a fantastic time at another party while we sit alone at ours. Our enthusiasm for our project turns as cold as platters of untouched meatballs. But the real reason people aren't making a conga line for our door is because we haven't gone out and dragged them to us. A less poetic but more helpful motto would be, "After you build it, work it so they will come."

Without follow-through, you can draft the business plan, lease the office space, print up business cards, buy the latest equipment, design a great website, and still go bust. You can call meeting after meeting to talk about plans for improvements at work, and find that nothing ever changes. You can spend months researching home exchanges in Italy and never set foot on Italian soil.

Adam had come close to the brink. So he took a risk. He threw his assumptions out the window and followed a bold plan of action that required him to be a lot more assertive (and much less comfortable) in seeking new business. He started doing more hard sell. He took a leap and invested some of his savings in advertising. He joined forces with a partner. When that relationship ended after a year, he hired an employee who had programming skills that allowed Adam to diversify in ways he had never anticipated. He eventually developed a popular software program for a niche market.

Adam never would have arrived at his current situation if he hadn't dared to venture along a path that he hadn't walked before, without a clue about what might happen around the next corner. He had to problem-solve every time he came up against an obstacle, and he typically had no alternative but to do that by trial and error. However, if he had waited for luck to make things happen, there's a good chance he'd still be waiting.

The bottom line is that you need follow-through to make anything happen for you. Imagine that your idea is like a beautiful bike. You admire it, polish it, tinker with it, spin its wheels over and over again. But if you want it to take you anywhere, you have to get on it and ride. Follow-through is the ride that brings a part of you and the bike to life. During the ride, you may fall off more than once, going up hills may be tough, going down hills may be scary, you may hit some obstacles and have to detour. But there are two things you can be sure of. The first is that you will get somewhere you want to go. The second is that as you pedal, there will be times when you feel like you're flying.

CUE CARD

- The worst thing that happens to those who fall short in follow-through is nothing. That's it. Nothing happens. Life goes on as is. But for those who do have an ambition, follow-through is what you need to make it happen.

- Follow-through isn't a to-do list; it's an adventurous, gutsy state of mind. It's the mindset required to venture towards a destination when you're not quite sure how to get from here to there.

- Commitment is an essential part of a plan but it only gets you to the starting gate. And to get to where you want, you can't afford to count on luck. You must be prepared to keep moving forward, even when you have no idea what may await you around the next corner.

- While you can't know exactly how your journey will unfold, and you could run into a few detours en route, you can be sure that if you persist, you'll arrive.

TWO

Yes, but I don't believe in myself

Consider follow-through as a road you decide to travel without being entirely sure of what's around the next corner. As you stand there at the beginning of a path with no end in sight, you may have a flash of concern that you're about to make a big mistake. What if you don't get to where you want to go, what if your big idea lands you in an outpost cubicle by the exit door, surrounded by backstabbers and stapler stealers? Suddenly your Uncle Bob's finger-wagging warning, "Better safe than sorry," seems worthy of consideration. You used to think he was pathologically risk-averse, but now you're not so sure that his way isn't the smarter way. Seriously, you may ask yourself, why not relinquish this ambition and continue on as before? Things weren't that bad, after all.

You could give up on following through on your ambition and stick with the tried and true, or you could ignore Uncle Bob yet again and start walking. So what is it you need to push you off the fence? Two things: faith in yourself, and more faith in yourself.

It's not news that in order to succeed we need to believe in ourselves. We know confidence is power. That's why so many of us stand in front of the mirror in the safety of our bathrooms and give ourselves phenomenal pep talks. Who among us hasn't declared to our reflection, "God, I'm good." But it's one thing to stand there waving a toothbrush and feeling like a conqueror; it's another to open the door, move out into the real world, and barrel assuredly past obstacles to showcase your talent to the world. The kind of confidence that is able to withstand the skeptics and the trip-ups that are waiting beyond the bathroom door is built on something more than a wink in the mirror. It's built on faith in yourself.

To believe in yourself, first and foremost, you have to have faith in yourself. So goes the wisdom since biblical times, when it was said, "Have faith and ye shall believe." To illustrate the point, faith is the horse that pulls the cart, the soil in which you plant the seeds, the protein that builds the muscle. The metaphors are endless but they all give rise to the same question: how exactly do you get this heavy-duty faith in yourself?

For the answer, I consulted the experts. I turned to priests, rabbis, Zen masters, Buddhist teachers, philosophers, and a few channellers for good measure. Sadly, not one could offer me a twelve-step program for gaining faith and influencing destiny. The best they could do was explain what faith is, and what it's not. To sum up these sages, here's what faith isn't:

Faith is not wishful thinking

You can stick your lottery ticket to your forehead and chant your numbers three times a day, but that won't make it a winner. You can uncross those fingers, toes, and eyes now. Simply wanting something to be true won't make it so. Blast and darn.

Faith is not about blind pursuit

If you become tongue-tied at dinner parties and witty come-backs only ever come to you in the middle of the night, you're not going to make it as the next David Letterman. If the position requires a degree in law and you think a tort is a fancy word for something that comes in a pie dish, don't quit your day job.

Faith is not hoping for divine intervention

It's not about sitting around playing online solitaire or build-ing Eiffel Towers with matchsticks while waiting for a sign. For those of us who always check our email and phone mes-sages with great expectation, this is the cruellest blow of all.

Here's what faith is:

Faith is trust in real possibility

It's having reason to believe your goal is worthy, and that you can attain it. Sure, at this stage, you may lack knowledge and you may need to strengthen some skills, but, at your very core, you feel you can accomplish your ambition. You

25

know it's doable, certainly possible. It's within your control to make happen.

Faith is confidence you're doing the right thing

It's a certainty that in the end – no matter what – something worthwhile will come of your beliefs and actions. It's the feeling that pursuing this ambition is the best thing you can do for the person you are, and the person you want to be.

When you have faith in yourself, you don't require absolute proof of what will be, and you don't need the buy-in of others. The faith that will power you to follow through isn't built on certainty or even hope. Those with the follow-through factor say that what keeps them going is simply an unshakeable feeling that they're doing the right thing, and that in some way they'll like themselves more for it. They say that while it's frustrating to hit roadblocks, they feel better about themselves when they try to manoeuvre around the obstacles than when they give up. Faith comes down to personal fulfillment.

For the most part, we never have the luxury of knowing for sure what the tangible upshot of our efforts will be. But even if we forget about money or other measurable rewards, we can still have trust and confidence that our attempts to bring our idea to life will make our days more meaningful and interesting for us. We can be excited about the idea of moving forward into new terrain. We can know that whatever should happen, we'll like ourselves that much more for going after our goal. Some ideas are just worth pursuing because, in the pursuing, we get to be true to ourselves. Follow-through is the deal that you make with yourself to do right by who you are.

Faith is the DNA of follow-through. When you have a deep-seated feeling that you are doing the right thing in following your goal, you can be an unstoppable force. The key is that your conviction has to be genuinely heartfelt. In other words, while there's a lot in life we fake daily and well – like hysterical laughter over a friend's unfunny joke – we can't feign faith. You can't try to make yourself believe you want to achieve certain goals when, deep within, you couldn't care less. You can't lie to yourself and pretend you're interested in taking the steps required to achieve your objective when you secretly hope the project in question will evaporate into thin air.

You can't fake faith, because faith is an energizing, authentic feeling. If the only reason you're pursuing an interest is because it's the easiest of options, or because it seems like something you *should* be doing, then you'll be proceeding without the power of faith behind you. You won't have that sense that this is truly the right thing for you to do. And without that feeling, it's hard to get over an anthill, let alone a mountain that you perceive to be blocking your way. You won't keep a promise to yourself that you don't want to shake on.

27

NOTE TO SELF: People may tell you they know you better than you know yourself. They don't. Colleagues may prod you to take on an assignment because they "know" you'll feel good about earning additional money. Friends may dissuade you from participating in a program because they "know" it will stress you out. People hold opinions about you; they hold beliefs about what you ought to want or feel, but only you can know what truly excites or drains you. Always beware the words "ought to" – they often lead to empty actions. And empty actions are so called because they're devoid of real meaning for us.

The test of faith

To determine whether your faith is real, the priests, rabbis, and other spiritual teachers I consulted suggest you put it to the ultimate test. Ask yourself this: "Do I have sound reason for my faith?" I was surprised to learn that this was the end-of-the-year exam question. It seemed to me as if these sages expected people to supply advance proof of the success of their ambition. My wise consultants set me straight.

They explained that faith is about the relationship you have with yourself. And every good relationship is founded on trust and confidence. In religious terms, faith is about your relationship with your god; you trust in your belief, you have confidence in the value of your belief. In follow-through terms, faith is about your connection with yourself. You have confidence that you are doing the right thing by you, and you trust in your abilities to carry out that which is important to you. The question "Do you have sound reason for your faith?" asks you to consider what matters to you. In pursuing your goal, are you honouring who you are?

If your goal doesn't promote values or ideas that are meaningful to you, then you may not be able to access the trust and confidence you need to make that goal happen. What is the fire that will sustain you through thick and thin? Is it the belief that you are doing something worthwhile? If not, then perhaps you are driven by a need of some kind, maybe a need for recognition or money.

The problem with need is that it wears like too much perfume. We have to spritz ourselves long and hard with fake optimism, interest, and heartiness to mask the scent of our desperation. And we're still not fooling anyone. We admire people who have faith in themselves. We run as fast as we can from those who are needy.

The slew of talent shows on television drives home the point. During the audition phase, it's easy to spot the contestants who don't believe in what they're doing. And, as Simon Cowell makes so painfully clear on *American Idol,* these people are wasting our time. Faith impresses; empty actions leave us cold.

Ask anyone who has ever achieved a goal of any kind and they'll tell you the same thing: you've got to want it. Not need it, want it. And you want it when the idea of your going for it, at this very second, doesn't feel dutiful or terrifying, but electrifying and doable. You're excited to see what will happen. When you've got that feeling, you've got faith. And when you have faith, you have every reason to believe in your strength to follow through.

CUE CARD

- Faith is the DNA of follow-through. Faith is about the relationship you have with yourself, and like every good relationship it must be built on trust and confidence.

- You need to trust that pursuing your goal is worthy and the right thing for you to do, if for no other reason than you'll like yourself better for trying.

- You need to be confident that you can attain your goal, even if you have to pick up some skills and skirt around some obstacles to achieve it.

- You don't need a guarantee of success to develop the faith required to follow through; you only need the feeling that in pursuing your goal, you are honouring yourself.

THREE

Yes, but how do I know if my project is right for me?

I t's safe to say that if it were so easy for each of us to feel certain that we're doing the right thing in pursuing a goal, we'd all be setting out on our path, high-fiving each other along the way. It's not as if we're staying on Status Quo Road because we're just having so much darn fun doing the same old same old. No, the reason the follow-through-challenged stick to the trodden trail is because they don't know if they'll actually be better off for taking the road not travelled.

When Jill first came to my office, she whipped out from her briefcase a gigantic stack of folders bulging with papers, plunked them on my desk, and smiled with satisfaction.

"In these pages," Jill exclaimed, "you will find my exploration of myself."

It looked like someone had just dumped the contents of a filing cabinet on my desk.

Jill, an executive in market research, had been considering starting her own agency for five years. She contacted me to help her figure out whether it would be the right move for her. Since I'm a bit of a disorganized person who has never met a file I wanted to sort, I gathered up Jill's documents and placed them gingerly on her lap.

"Maybe you can capture the highlights for me?" I asked hopefully.

Jill thumbed through the dozens of personality profiles and quizzes she had taken over the years. As she flipped pages, she tossed out test scores and character attributes that would supposedly help her figure out what to do with her life.

Anticipating that Jill wanted to come up with an answer before the next century, I cut to the chase and asked, "What do you like to do in the course of a working day?"

This is an exquisitely simple question that's surprisingly effective.

Those with the follow-through factor confirm that this query serves up instant insight more easily and better than most. It doesn't ask you to contemplate what you want, or think you want. It doesn't ask what you hope for yourself, or don't hope. Instead, it works like a laser beam, high-lighting the elements that add up to time enjoyably spent. When you ask this question in the context of whether a project holds value for you, you'll find the points that spring to mind are useful guides.

Jill compiled a long list of activities she liked, including communicating with people, drawing up questions for focus groups, analyzing data, etc. She talked while I captured everything she said on a whiteboard.

Then I asked the key follow-up question, one that is less simple. Often this question triggers confusion and annoyance. I know it did for me when I was first asked it by a follow-through master. And it did for Jill.

"Why do you like . . ." I took up the first point on the whiteboard, "communicating with people?"

"Don't we all like to communicate?" replied Jill impatiently. I could tell she was thinking she should take her files and call someone else. "Aren't we social animals?"

I didn't go off track to discuss the two wordless dinner companions I had sat with at a recent wedding. Instead, I reframed the question so she could understand that the query was a tool to drill down to why she liked the activities that she did. "In relation to your work, what is it specifically that you like about the types of communications you have with people?"

"It interests me to find out what people think, and how they view their experience of a product or service," mused Jill. "I feel like a detective, trying to understand what motivates the consumer. It's fun."

Jill's enthusiasm picked up from there. For every activity she said she liked, she willingly ruminated over the question "Why?" And in doing so, she discovered she very much wanted the experience of running her own agency. She yearned to see if she could pull it off. If it failed and

33

she had to get a job again one day, she'd still be glad that she had given it a try.

Asking yourself *why* you like the things you do is a powerful way to get straight to the heart of whether it's meaningful for you to pursue an ambition. It's the surest path to understanding the root of your faith in your project.

My friend Kirsten started her career as an actress but eventually became a trainer and workshop leader instead. After she'd worked in theatre for several years, we talked about what she liked about acting and why she liked those things. At the time, Kirsten was casting around for more auditions and feeling drained by the search. During our conversation, she realized that she was putting a lot of effort into finding roles, yet stepping into a character every night wasn't very meaningful to her.

Kirsten was a musical theatre performer, but she discovered she didn't like entertaining for entertainment's sake. She wanted to be onstage to engage an audience and provoke them to new ways of thinking. She felt that didn't happen often in her line of work. It turned out that chasing after musical theatre roles wasn't the right plan; it wasn't linked to her true desires. She found a greater source of energy and determination in building her career as a workshop leader, where she could use her captivating talents to stimulate learning.

You know you're getting to the core of why something matters to you when you move from detailing an activity to describing the feelings it provokes. The easiest way to start the process is to break down your project into its smallest components. First, ask yourself whether you like each task. Then ask yourself *why* you like it, what is it that you feel when you're engaged in that activity. The exercise at the end of the chapter will help you have this conversation with yourself.

"Am I good enough?" is a trick question

You have faith in yourself when you have the confidence that in pursuing your project, you're strengthening your relationship with yourself. But faith is also founded on trust that you can achieve your goal. While you may conclude that it's meaningful for you to persevere, you can find yourself wondering if you have the right stuff to carry out your plan. It's not uncommon to ask yourself, "Am I good enough?" But that's a question that those with the follow-through factor warn against asking. It's a trick question, they say, one that has been known to bring a quick, unnecessary death to projects before they have had a chance to grow legs.

Assuming you have appropriate qualifications and a willingness to keep learning, the query "Am I good enough?" is meaningless. The answer changes as often as you change socks. When you do something impressive according to the standards of others, you feel hugely qualified. You can't help but admit to yourself that you are quite exceptional. Then you hit a bad day. You come up against a client who rolls his eyes at everything you say, your boss speaks to you as if you're a moron, or you hear people sing the praises of a not-

35

so-bright colleague. Suddenly, you're no longer confident that you're all that fantastic. You can drop from feeling competent to inadequate in about two seconds.

The question "Am I good enough?" asks that you compare yourself against a measure. But which measure will you use? In Jill's case, does she measure herself against a market research expert who has been in the business for two decades, has authored six books on the subject, and guest lectures at universities? Or does she compare herself to the guy who has much less experience than her and seems unable to sell pop to preteens?

There are always going to be people who are better than you and people who are worse, but that doesn't mean anything. Those with the follow-through factor are adamant that success doesn't require that you be the best in the world at whatever you want to do. It's not as if only extraordinary, highly experienced people in any industry manage to get business and everyone else must resort to washing dishes. Most people aren't award-winners yet are still able to meet client needs and earn promotions, in the same way that not all working musicians are virtuosos and not all published writers are J.K. Rowling.

The more helpful questions to strengthen trust in yourself are "Do I have a foundation of knowledge to build on? And if I don't, am I interested in developing one?"

In my case, I had the idea of starting a theme-cake business percolating at the back of my mind for years. It's a favourite pasttime of mine to moon over glossy cookbooks, examining pictures of gorgeous cakes, and in a moment of sugar-induced optimism, I once invested $125 plus tax in a professional decorating kit that came with an icing cone and a zillion confusing attachments.

Every cake I have ever made has come out of the oven looking like a ski slope. Every flower I have ever squeezed out of my icing cone looks like it's been regurgitated by a cow. I have never managed to scrawl more than "Happy Bir" before running out of room on a cake.

Does this mean I shouldn't pursue my idea for my home-based bakery? When I put that question to my husband, he looked askance at his birthday cake, which admittedly had a small crater in the middle of it (to symbolize the slippery slope of life, I argued), and didn't stop laughing until I flung a scoop of ice cream at his head. "Do you really think it would be such a smart idea?" I heard him mutter as he was towelling off.

It's always smart to follow through on a genuine interest, if only for these two reasons:

1. The world doesn't need another grouch

Opting to dispense with an interest in favour of sticking to a tedious grind can leave you feeling as if you are slowing sinking in quicksand. Naturally, this does nothing for your mood. Remaining disgruntled is a lot easier than trying something different, but you're not doing anyone a favour by taking the easy way out. Miserable people are no different than mosquitoes. There are too many of them, their whine drives you crazy, and worse, they can make you sick. The only thing the world wants to do with a mosquito, or a grump, is swat it very hard with a rolled-up newspaper.

2. Interesting work is better for you

Cher said it best when she said, "I've been rich, and I've been poor, and rich is better. I've been young, and I've been old, and young is better." If you've worked at something you like and you've worked at something you don't, you know that doing work you like is better. Doing what you enjoy energizes you. It really doesn't matter what you want to do; as long as it gives you a boost, it's worth a shot. As philosopher-poet Kahlil Gibran so famously said, "All work is empty save when there is love." If you engage in a project that interests you, you're a happier person.

Given these undeniable facts, when asked the question "Is it smart for you to pursue something you love doing?" there is only one rational answer: "Yes, of course it is." The more telling questions that my husband should have asked to avoid butterscotch ripple in his hair were, "What do you like about being a baker? Why do you like those things?" After answering those questions, I'd be able to determine whether I had reasons to trust in my ability to carry out my ambition.

What part of the baking process do I like? The eating of the cake. Do I enjoy making the cake? Not so much. That fact hit me on the head like a sack of flour the day I had to bake forty-eight cupcakes, each inscribed with a letter, for my daughter's class. By cupcake number twelve, I was getting a tad impatient. By cupcake number nineteen, I was smushing letters on with my finger to hurry the process along.

As I explore what I like and don't like about baking, I quickly determine that I lack a key ingredient for following through on my idea of starting a theme baking company: faith. This idea doesn't connect me to my personal values. I don't have reason to believe this is a meaningful course of action for me. As for my trust in my ability to make this project come to life, I have none. I don't have a foundation of knowledge to take me to the starting line. That's not necessarily a deal-breaker; I could learn what I need to. But I don't have trust because I don't have any desire or interest in learning.

To recap, trust and confidence are born when:

You know what is true for you

You are genuinely interested and engaged by the work that your project requires. To use Jill as an example, she's stimulated by the science of market surveys and the challenge of analyzing data. To use me as an example, I buy my icing in a can and don't bother reading the ingredients.

You know what you can do, and you are interested in developing your skill

39

Jill has a solid grasp on the logistics of running an agency but knows she needs to learn more about hiring and managing staff. She's motivated and interested to learn. For my part,

I know I'd spend my time in a baking class worrying about whether I was going to have to scrub pans at the end of it.

You want to climb the mountain just because it's there
Going up baby step by baby step may get frustrating and the path may seem endless, but even worse would be not to climb at all. Jill would be disappointed with herself if she never tried to start her own agency. In my case, I'm happy to stay put and flip through pictures of other people's achievements in the kitchen.

CUE CARD

- Understanding how activities link to your interests and values is the surest path to understanding the root of your faith in your idea.

- The easiest way to start the process is to break down your project into its smallest components. First, ask yourself whether you like each task, and then ask why. What is it that you feel when you're engaged in the activity?

- Avoid asking yourself whether you're "good enough" to carry off your plan. Assuming you have appropriate qualifications and a willingness to keep learning, that query is meaningless. The more helpful questions to strengthen trust in your ability are "Do I have a foundation of knowledge to build on? And if I don't, am I interested in developing one?"

A short conversation about what's right for you

There are a few key questions you can ask yourself to help clarify whether you believe following through on your idea is the right move for you at this time.

The challenge when talking things over with yourself is to avoid defaulting to habitual responses. One client illustrated this standard pitfall when he said, "Why should I bother talking to myself? I already know what I'm thinking."

There's a world of difference between a pat response to a question you ask yourself and true reflection. Giving yourself a customary answer is like switching on an automatic pilot button. It will get you to where you have always gone before. When you reflect on your response, you override all pre-programming.

To help you have a different and more contemplative dialogue with yourself, try this exercise. Imagine you are far from home, travelling through the night on a train. There is only one other person in your compartment, a stranger who radiates wisdom and kindness. After a while, you strike up a conversation. You know you will never see this person again and that knowledge frees you to be as honest as you would like. Complete the sentences in this conversation with the traveller.

41

You: There's something I've always told myself I would like to do.

Traveller: What is it?

You: I've always wanted to . . .

_____

_____

_____

Traveller: Why is that meaningful to you?

You: I suppose because I . . .

_____

_____

_____

Traveller: Is there another reason why it matters?

You: Deep down, I want . . .

_____

_____

_____

Traveller: You know, as you follow through on your idea, you are likely going to come up against some obstacles. What do you think these obstacles will be?

You: I anticipate . . .

_____

_____

_____

Traveller: Is the desire to achieve your goal greater than the obstacles you will have to overcome to do so?
You:

_____

_____

_____

Traveller: Let me ask you this: How would you feel about yourself if you didn't follow through on your aspiration?
You: I think I'd feel . . .

_____

_____

_____

Traveller: You can do it, you know. It's just a matter of making a deal with yourself that you will. Signing on the dotted line is the first step . . .

....

Your signature   *Date*

FOUR

Yes, but I don't know what's true for me

S ometimes you just can't be sure what you want. You think you know, but you're open to the possibility of being wrong. As a matter of fact, you can talk yourself in and out of what you want on a dime. Nobody yo-yos better and faster with the word "maybe" than you do.

"I think I want to do this project, but maybe I don't. Maybe I could find something better to do. Maybe I should stop talking to myself and go to a movie."

Don't make the mistake of thinking that because you're a yo-yo master you are indecisive and don't know your own mind. You're not wishy-washy, you're simply overcome by truths. You see truth in every side of the argument that you have with yourself. For good reason – there isn't one authoritative, overriding truth to guide you.

There isn't even a single, universally agreed-upon definition of truth. Over the years, I have come across a migraine-inducing number of different interpretations from philosophers, scientists, lawyers, and writers. The only thing most of these heavy-weight thinkers more or less agree upon is that truth is subjective.

Those who argue that there is such a thing as objective truth would be wasting their breath, particularly when trying to convince philosophers. As a group, philosophers make the case that objective truth, which is based on observable unbiased data, is true only in a particular time and place. Change the time and place, and what we thought was inarguably true no longer is.

Until the summer of 2006, every astronomy textbook and science teacher insisted that Pluto was a planet. Since then, it has lost planet status. When you read through the list of achievements of Nobel Prize–winning physicists, you find that every second one is honoured for devising a means of superconductivity or fusion beyond what was "previously believed possible." With facts changing from indisputable to disproved on a regular basis, it's no wonder we're a tad insecure about Crazy-Gluing ourselves to a so-called truth.

Since our truth is forever altering, it can be tough to consistently claim that pursuing a particular idea is the best thing for us do to. As the philosophers say, truth can only be defined as perspective. And perspectives shift, depending on where you stand in a particular time and place. So, one day the truth is that it's right for you to damn the torpedoes and go after your ambition, and the next day you see things differently.

45

A lot of people wrestle with this dilemma, but I doubt that few have wrestled with it more than I have. If there were an award for the world's best flip-flopper, I'd have a trophy case full of them. I was good at dithering. Very, very good. I was so adept at seeing things from different points of view, I could never stay true to any one perspective for long.

My way of being, for a mind-blowing number of years, could be described in one word: torn. I was torn about everything, including, ironically, the writing of a book on follow-through. I'd like to say the idea for this book came to me a respectful three years ago, but honestly it popped into my head long before we hit the new millennium. It was about twelve years ago that I first realized that the follow-through factor was the missing link between desire and achievement. At the time, I thought I'd like to write about my discovery.

However, was my truth that I wanted to dedicate after-work hours to this project? It was a fact that I believed in the idea, and it held enormous appeal for me. But wasn't it also true that I wanted to devote all my after-work hours to my family? And wasn't it true that while I wanted to write a book about the follow-through factor, I also wanted to write magazine articles on other topics? If I were being honest, would I not say that I could see value in all my options?

Any time I had an idea for my life, I would cross-examine myself mercilessly until I begged myself for a bathroom break. As a matter of fact, my skill as a self-intimidating interrogator prompted me to half-consider going into law. But that led to yet another cross-examination that left me, as usual, torn.

Thankfully, the follow-through factor can be learned. And I learned it. My research showed that the only way to end my pattern of wavering was to redefine truth. Those who follow through don't think of truth as a valid perspective, but as a source of positive energy. There is truth in every perspective. But does every perspective give you the same energy charge? That's the question for flip-floppers to ask themselves.

It's a life-changing question, but what do you do when the answer doesn't spring readily to mind? Some people are extremely attuned to even the slightest surges and dips in their energy levels, while others among us aren't born with much of an internal Richter scale. Interestingly, in almost every case, the body transmits loud signals when we're making decisions we clearly don't want to make. Some form of physical or mental distress nearly always attaches itself to an undesired course of action. You put an offer on a house that everyone says you should love, but instead of feeling excited, you feel ill. You decide to stop freelancing and go after a regular nine-to-five job, but when an employer calls with an offer of a full-time gig, you want to fling yourself off the nearest bridge. Likewise, we are physically electrified by those big, exciting decisions that are so right for us.

However, most of the day-to-day choices we need to make to follow through just aren't big enough to switch us on or off. When your body isn't giving you any clues, the solution is to ask yourself the following three questions to uncover the energy that lurks inside every choice:

1. Why do I want to make this idea happen?

Often when you've held an ambition in the back of your mind for a long time, it crystallizes into something like an iceberg. You think and talk about the idea, but only superficially. You address the tip of your idea. It's important to go deep and ask yourself what's beneath that tip. What is it about your idea that makes you want to follow through on it today?

Santos was a busy architect who was frustrated with himself for not following through with long-held plans to go back to school part-time for a degree in archaeology. When asked why he wanted to get that degree, he drew a blank.

"I guess because I always said I'd do it," answered Santos. "I don't have any other reason when I think about it."

"Does the idea of spending your evenings in lecture halls and doing assignments excite you at all?" I wondered.

"Not one little bit," replied Santos. "Well," he added happily, "I guess I can stop beating myself up now."

2. Are there other ways to achieve what I want?

After you determine why you want to pursue your plan, con-sider if there are other ways to give yourself what you're look-ing for. Santos recognized that there were alternative means for him to indulge his interest in archaeology, other than going to school. He got a kick out of the idea of joining a museum-sponsored expedition or taking a volunteer vacation where he could work on a dig.

In my case, I had started working with clients and holding workshops on the follow-through factor, but to help a greater number of people achieve their ambition, I couldn't think of any other option but to write a book. It was the only choice that would move me closer to my own professional goals.

3. What's the price I'll pay?

This question acknowledges the fact that every action requires some kind of investment, not necessarily of money, but certainly of time, focus, and energy. So what is the cost to you to pursue the idea, and how does your stom-ach react to that cost? The flip side of this question is what's the cost of not pursuing your plan? And how does your stomach respond?

Santos's gut spoke out loud and clear on this question. He didn't feel good at all about the thought of investing thou-sands of dollars and huge amounts of time into another degree. But he had no issue with spending holiday money on an organized expedition.

49

This was also a great question for me. In answering, I found I was upset at the idea of extending my workdays, since that would mean spending less time with my young daughter. At the same time, putting off this book was making me mad at myself. There was only one option that didn't bring me down, and that was to revisit my daily schedule to fit in at least a little time for writing, even if that meant turning away some work opportunities.

These particular questions bring to the surface the energy that the options hold for you. You'll find you're invigorated by some of your answers and deflated or even downright bored by others. Those with the follow-through factor know that the only thing to do when confronted with different perspectives, all of which are valid, is to follow the energy.

When you ask yourself reflective questions such as "Why do I want to make this idea happen?" don't stop at the first answer you come up with, but drill down as much as you can. Follow every one of your answers with "Why?" Say you decide you want to change careers. Ask yourself, "What are ten reasons why I want to do this?" I often push clients to come up with eleven answers to a single question. People typically start to struggle beyond the sixth answer, but it's only after you run out of easy, obvious responses that your thinking goes deeper and you get to the core of the issue.

CUE CARD

- Typically, truth is defined as a valid perspective. But perspectives change depending on where you're standing at a particular time and place.

- When contemplating whether to follow through on an idea, you may flip-flop between perspectives. At that point, the only way forward is to define truth as a source of positive energy. After all, there's truth in every perspective, but does every perspective give you the same surge of energy? If you can't determine which option gives you the most charge, ask yourself these three questions:

  1. Why do I want this idea to happen?
  2. Are there other ways to achieve what I want?
  3. What's the price I'll pay?

- Elaborate on your answers and you'll feel the energy that lurks inside the choice.

How to stop yourself from flip-flopping

Flip-floppers aren't wishy-washy. Instead, we have a great talent for seeing things from different perspectives. But this same talent can be our undoing if we find ourselves hopping from side to side on every issue instead of moving forward.

When you're dithering endlessly over the question "What is true for me?" the only thing to do is to change the question. Ask yourself instead, "What gives me the greatest charge of energy?"

To help you determine whether following through on your ambition will invigorate you, ask yourself these five telling questions:

1. **Why do I want to make this idea happen?**
   (Consider whether it is still important for you to bring your idea to life.)

   _____

   _____

   _____

   _____

   _____

   _____

   _____

2. **Are there other ways to achieve what I want?**
   (*Determine whether there are alternative, and perhaps
   preferable, options to get the same results.*)

   _____

   _____

   _____

   _____

   _____

   _____

   _____

   _____

3. **What's the price I'll pay for following through on my
   ambition?** (*Assess the time, money, or energy you will need
   to invest.*)

   _____

   _____

   _____

   _____

   _____

   _____

   _____

   _____

   _____

4. What's the price I'll pay for not following through on my ambition?

_____

_____

_____

_____

_____

_____

_____

_____

5. What gives me a greater surge of energy – the idea of following through on my ambition or the idea of letting it go?

_____

_____

_____

_____

_____

_____

_____

_____

FIVE

Yes, but what's the point?

S am is a skeptic, a pursed-lipped downer who, over the years, has mastered the twin arts of grimacing and eye-rolling. And there are millions of Sams in all shapes and sizes, shrugging, frowning, looking up to the ceiling, shaking their heads at every idea we have. Just as the inner critic is a fact of life, external detractors are also unavoidable. You can't escape them. Count on at least one scowling doubter looking over your shoulder at your office, at your mother's house, at your gym, at your local watering hole.

You can't run and you can't hide from a naysayer Sam because you no sooner duck one pessimistic know-it-all than another pops up to tell you that your idea is doomed. Stand in line at a coffee house long enough and you can observe a Sam sidling up to some innocent man or woman whom he happened to have met for five minutes at a party.

"So," says the Sam. "It's Tuesday afternoon and you're not working. Won the lottery, did you?" This is a typical attempt on the part of a Sam to provoke unease.

"Well, I'm working for myself now so I have my own hours. I've just started my own company," the person might reply politely.

"Really? What kind of business?" asks the Sam.

"An online catalogue company."

"Ah. Interesting." A pause will follow while the Sam sifts quickly through a very large internal databank of bad news to find just the right tidbit to burst the person's bubble.

"You know, I recently read something about online catalogue companies," the Sam will say. The increased energy in a Sam's voice is your clue that a person is about to get hit with a damning fact. "Apparently, the fad is over."

Wait for it. More unsubstantiated so-called facts are about to come flying. "I gather, at one point, everyone was setting up these types of businesses, but now they've all gone bankrupt. I understand if you don't have an enormous marketing budget, it's practically impossible to survive. Do you do a lot of advertising?"

"Uh, no, not so much really."

"Oh. That's a shame." And now . . . the grimace accompanied by a shrug. "Well, good luck to you." With that, the Sam will move forward to greet the barista, satisfied that he has once again managed to spread a little gloom in his wake.

Encounters with Sams always end the same way. We're left standing alone with a weak smile plastered on our face, wondering for the tenth, hundredth, thousandth time, if our efforts really are worth the bother. It's at moments like these that we slide over to the dark side.

Anyone who has ever struggled with follow-through has visited the dark side more than once. It's a grim place where not a lot happens. Well, nothing at all happens there, actually. That's why it's the dark side. This place has a name: it's called Pointless.

Welcome to Pointless

You've got a project, an idea, a plan, and you have good reason to believe you can make it work. You'd love to do it. The project makes you feel up, gives you energy. You start mapping it out, fleshing out a few ideas. You're starting to turn sod when suddenly you notice a big sign. It reads: Welcome to Pointless. And that's when so many throw down the shovel and pick up their lives where they left off.

The world already has umpteen stars in every field imaginable. Great producers, programmers, gamers, actors, renovators, entrepreneurs, broadcasters, builders, publishers, sales reps, writers, painters, carpenters . . . the list is virtually endless. What have you got to offer that's so special, so original? There are hundreds of people already doing what you want to do, and they're doing a great job at it. When you look around and see what's out there already, all your efforts can seem a little, or a lot, pointless.

"The world doesn't need me," you might say to a Sam, who, in this instance, could be your stick-in-the-mud friend who hasn't changed her hair, let alone her life, in twenty years.

"No one is indispensable," this Sam would surely condescend.

You swallow your drink and descend into silent gloom. A bored Sam will sigh, "We can't all be big fish in the sea."

"Why should I even bother getting into the sea at all?" you moan. "There are more than enough designers out there."

"That's true," she'll readily agree. "If you ask me, I think you're crazy to even think about going for it. Big waste of time, money, effort. What's the point?"

Those with the follow-through factor say there is only one point – personal interest.

We can't always easily justify our own particular interest. Why does a tired fifty-five-year-old lawyer want to move heaven and earth to fit adult ballet classes into her life? It's not as if she's got a snowball's chance of getting hired by the New York City Ballet. Why does a forty-four-year-old flash animator decide to take a securities course? Why does a straightlaced fifty-nine-year-old civil servant invest real money in recording his songs and a video for MySpace? Asking us to rationalize our personal inclinations is like asking us to describe the taste of vanilla. It's unknowable to anyone but the person who tastes it. Our interests are strictly our own, they make up a part of who we are, and when we pursue our interest, we shake hands with ourselves. Our life becomes richer, more colourful. And that's the ultimate point.

58 When you follow through, you acquire experiences that lift you out of your everyday routine. You meet people you might otherwise never have met, and you hold new, different conversations. You challenge yourself to come up with solutions

when you encounter obstacles and you allow the unexpected into your life. If this sounds like material for a good story, it's because it is. Show up for your idea, and you are guaranteed some sort of an adventure.

The only point of anything is the point we give it

When it comes to thinking about a rock-hard reason to carry on with your ambition, look inside, not outside. The only point of anything is the point we give it.

The world isn't holding its breath for any of us to create new art or launch new businesses or services. Unless you've got the cure for cancer or a way to save the environment, no one is desperate for what you have to offer. Hopefully, whatever you want to do will contribute positively to a few or a lot of people, but if you chose to drop out of life to live in a remote fishing cabin, the world would go on.

You can be sure that whatever it is that you are proposing is already being offered in some form or another. But that's not cause to shred the napkin on which you so excitedly scribbled your concept. Of course, you need to consider the competition and market needs. It's possible that you'll have to adapt your idea to make it more desirable or viable. But these aren't issues to deliberate when determining if there's a big-picture point for proceeding at all.

The only thing you need to consider is the value of your ambition to yourself. Start off easy by listing personal benefits that success could bring to you. Ask yourself, "What's in it for me?" Would you gain greater control over your life, be involved in more engaging activities, exercise your creativity, earn more money, learn a new skill, etc.? Next, think about what you hope your project would bring to other people's lives. It doesn't have to be life-altering. At the very least, a happier you will be a boost to those in your world.

Joe, who worked in human resources, told me he wanted to be a photographer. But he worried, "There are so many professional photographers out there. And every amateur with a digital camera thinks they're a pro. What's the point of my getting into photography? When I look at the numbers, my idea seems just plain dumb. I bet you know a dozen starving photographers yourself."

I didn't. I listed off the photographers I did know. I had a client who had established herself as a specialist in children's black-and-white portraits. Her travelling exhibit had recently moved into my local coffee house and she had enough commissions to afford a nanny three days a week. I remembered that a friend had had a session with an ego-destroying photographer who told her to keep her chin up so it wouldn't look so recessive. She wouldn't be recommending him to anyone. I had met others while working at magazines and newspapers. But on the whole, I could name a lot more hairdressers, dentists, and doctors. And writers. And coaches. I could name dozens and dozens of those.

"It doesn't matter who else is out there," I insisted. "If you're looking for an empty playing field, forget it. You won't find one anywhere. So if you feel good about your talent and you want to be a photographer, then be a photographer."

"And starve?"

"Joe, you're frustrated because you're an HR specialist who yearns to be a photographer. So right now, as of this minute, flip it around. Be a photographer who has a job as an HR specialist. Think like a photographer, act like a photographer, and see what happens."

Joe and I brainstormed how he could showcase his work at the office and let employees in his large company know that he was available to take pictures.

"We can detail a step-by-step plan," I told Joe. "But the very first step is for you to give yourself permission to be a photographer."

"And you don't think that's pointless?"

"How does it feel to think of yourself as a photographer, to call yourself a photographer?"

"I love it; it feels great. I feel like I've got a new lease on life."

"Do you feel you can take pictures that will be meaningful to you and to other people?"

"No question about that. People really connect with my work."

"Then a photographer who has his own unique vision and talent is born. Welcome to the world you want to play in – there's always room for one more."

Competition is a fact of life. If a lot of people are already doing what you want to do, that just proves there's a market for it. And even if you don't feel you can do anything better than some others, you can be sure that at least you will do *something* differently.

For follow-through, it's critical to remember that no two people are exactly alike, which means you bring a unique twist to whatever you offer. The service or product you want to sell may be a clone of something that already exists, but the way you go about pitching it to the market has to be different by the very fact that no one else is you. The book you may want to write may already be on the market in some form or another, but your manuscript will be the only one that is a reflection of you and your choices.

Those who follow through do so for no other reason than they want to see where their personal interest will take them. As the legendary actress Ethel Barrymore said, "That's all there is; there isn't any more."

CUE CARD

- Don't look outside yourself to determine the point of any project or ambition. The issue isn't whether the world needs you to make your idea happen, but whether *you* need to make your idea happen to make your life more interesting.
- Nothing has meaning but the meaning you give it. If it's worthwhile to you, that's the whole point of going for it.
- It doesn't matter that other people are successfully offering the same service or product that you wish to offer. We live in a copycat culture where goods and services are cloned by the second. But you can't clone a human. What you bring to the playing field is your individual uniqueness. That's your true value added.

How to determine the point

It can take a skeptical Sam less than a minute to dismiss your idea as redundant.

Before you even finish outlining your concept, Sam will tell you that it's already being done by many people who are more knowledgeable and better financed than you. And so you lie awake in the early hours of the morning wrestling with the question, "What's the point of bothering?"

You won't find your answer on Google. All you'll find online are lists of websites that are advertising products or services similar to your own. Nowadays, good ideas get cloned by the second. But fortunately, while people's ideas rarely remain unique for long, individuals themselves are always inimitable. Whatever you do, you will do differently than others, if only because you aren't a carbon copy of anyone.

In any case, the question to ask yourself is not whether the world needs your project, but whether *you* need your project to make your life more interesting and enjoyable. To help you arrive at an answer so you can finally sleep through the night, jot down your responses to the queries below.

1. *How will following through on your ambition change your life for the better?*

_____

_____

_____

_____

2. *How will fulfilling your goal help other people, directly or indirectly?*

_____

_____

_____

_____

_____

3. *What is one thing you would do differently from anyone else in your field?*

_____

_____

_____

_____

_____

_____

4. *Complete this sentence: It's worth it to follow through if only because . . .*

_____

_____

_____

_____

SIX

Yes, but I have five ideas and all of them are great

Pity the follow-through-challenged who are intelligent, talented, and creative. They are plagued by choices, tormented by opportunities. The harsh truth is that too much of a good thing can be a problem. You can be too thin, at tax time you can be too rich, and you can be weighed down by too many ideas. Multi-talented people with options galore can be among the most miserable people you'll ever meet. And the most paralyzed.

I was once seated at a dinner party across from a dynamo named Chloe and her pal Mark. Sitting between them was a poor man whose head was whipping from side to side faster than a tennis ball at Wimbledon as he looked from Chloe to Mark while they talked about what Chloe should do with her life.

"I had an amazing week," Chloe said, while tearing her dinner roll to shreds.

"Great. Did you find an office to rent?" asked Mark.

"No, no. Maybe something better. A friend asked me to collaborate on a book project about social marketing."

"You're going to publish a book now?" Mark sounded skeptical. The man trapped in between looked interested.

"Well, once I get out a book, I could hold seminars about how to market online."

"Do you want to do that?" asked Mark.

"Sure, why not? I'd be a good presenter."

"But last week you were going to really focus on building up a new business. And now you're going to concentrate on writing a book?" exclaimed Mark. The man in the middle tut-tutted.

"I don't know. A former colleague who's working at a business college says she'll put in a good word for me if I want to apply for a teaching position."

"Okay, that sounds like a plan," said Mark. "But what about . . ."

"Oh, I forgot to tell you. I met this guy who works at the Shopping Channel. I showed him the carry-all that I made that has the dozen hidden pockets. He loved it. He said he thought it would sell like crazy. I could make a fortune. I'm thinking of putting together a business plan, then looking for an investor. What do you think?"

"Sounds interesting," said Mark. The man in the middle looked dubious.

"Really?" asked Chloe.

"Why not?" Mark said. "Hey, did you ever call that TV producer you met about getting some freelance work as a researcher?"

At this point, the man in the middle insisted that he swap seats so that Chloe could sit next to Mark. With their heads now close together, I could no longer eavesdrop. But I had no doubt where Chloe's story was going. Nowhere. There is nothing like playing with options to keep you spinning your wheels.

When you're trying to follow through on something, having other appealing opportunities pop up fast and furious is downright agonizing. It's not that we fear that our original idea will prove to be a terrible mistake, but we're terrified that these other possibilities could turn out to be even better.

Many with follow-through challenges fit the profile of a "maximizer," a term coined by Barry Schwartz in his book *The Paradox of Choice*. Maximizers want to be sure they're getting the very best of everything, from jeans to spouses to jobs. They are known as the world's most tireless shoppers, motivated by the belief that if they just keep looking, they will find perfection. You don't have to look far to spot a maximizer. They're the ones climbing back and forth over your knees at the movie theatre in their quest for a better seat. You see them in hotel hallways rolling their suitcase from room to room, determined to find the one with the best mattress, farthest from the ice-maker. Though to the rest of the world the maximizer can seem insanely picky, and to go shoe shopping with one takes years off your life, maximizers are not unreasonable sorts, at least not in their own minds. They aren't ridiculously demanding, they are simply extreme optimists. They have a feeling that something better exists and they fear settling for less than the best.

The drawback is that this particular brand of optimism leaves you feeling dissatisfied, frustrated, and fearful of taking a step in any direction. If there was no choice, you wouldn't have to worry about making one that was less than perfect, whereas having too many options can backfire, as shown in the study "When Choice Is Demotivating" by Sheena S. Iyengar at Columbia University and Mark R. Lepper at Stanford University. In one instance, the researchers set up a sample table of six jars of exotic jams in a gourmet shop, and a sample table of twenty-four types of jam in another. It turns out that the more choice people had, the less jam they bought. Sales at the smaller table were up twenty-seven percent over sales at the larger sample table. It's easier to turn your back on fruit spreads altogether than fret over whether to go with gooseberry peach, apricot lemon, cherry banana, or twenty-one possibly even better concoctions.

Those who are talented and resourceful face a similar dilemma of sorts. When you sit back and contemplate what you "might" do, the possibilities suddenly seem overwhelming. Once the creative juices start to flow, ideas tend to bubble up in clusters, making it hard to decide which ones to pop and which to pursue.

David, a Hollywood-based freelance writer, sought me out when he was paralyzed by indecision. Should he stick to writing a screenplay on spec or put his energies into writing a pilot for a tv-producer friend, developing a play for a promising theatre troupe looking for new talent, or joining an ad agency that was offering him a position? For David, the problem was that he wasn't thinking about the actual jobs, he was fast-forwarding to imagined outcomes. He liked the idea of himself as a successful screenwriter or playwright. Then again, the steady paycheque of a jet-setting power ad exec conjured up appealing pictures of a life lived in Hugo Boss suits.

We all tend to get carried away with images of ourselves arriving at the finish line to cheering crowds. But here's where reality hits, and hurts. In real life, we never actually reach our red ribbon, because we keep pushing it forward a few feet. It would be great if David became an established screenwriter or playwright and had assignments drop into his lap. But professional success doesn't wipe out ongoing work anxieties. After you score once, you feel even greater pressure to live up to expectations and score again. Say David chooses to work with the ad agency. He might make a six-figure salary, but he'll feel the heat to retain key clients.

In the same way that ads can have us believe that a particular car is our ticket to open-road freedom, we think that if we just pick the right opportunity, we'll arrive at some sort of Utopia. But not even a Ferrari can fly through rush-hour traffic, and no type of work can take you to Shangri-La, let alone keep you there.

We are not creatures who hang out for long periods in an uninterrupted state of delight. That's because, for good or bad, we are a highly adaptable species. Novelty wears off quickly and in a short time we inevitably return to the business of daily life, with all its inherent hassles and irritations. There's a famous study that asked accident victims who were left paralyzed and people who had won lotteries to rate their happiness level about a year after the event. The lottery winners proved to be no happier than people in general. The accident victims, while somewhat less happy than most people, still judged themselves to be happy, largely because they were coping better than they had expected. It is human nature to adjust to circumstances, be these good or difficult.

So for those trying to choose between equally interesting possibilities, the good news is that it truly doesn't matter which one you pick. Behind every door there is something of value, but not one will lead to the perfect life. Barry Schwartz's recommendation for making choices in a world of abundant options is to set a personal standard of "good enough" rather than the always elusive "best." That's exactly what those with the follow-through factor do.

Good enough is not second-best. It's a green light to go with whatever meets your non-negotiable criteria. In David's case, he came to realize that he wanted to spend his days writing comedy. The job with the ad company didn't fit the

71

bill. The others did. In the end, he committed to writing a pilot for a comedy series. He might have been equally happy writing for a theatre troupe, but he tilted towards the television gig because he thought he'd have the most fun riffing ideas with his producer pal.

Throw out the list of pros and cons

Standard wisdom has you write a list of pros and cons for each ambition you have. That's great in theory, but in practice these lists are as useful as expired Aspirins. And God knows, you'll need full-strength Aspirin to get through the exercise. Most of us don't have the time or inclination to spend weeks researching the ups and downs of every possibility we dream up, so instead of compiling accurate lists, we string together assumptions based on our limited knowledge.

Here's how it works: Every time I call my friend who teaches at college, he's at home stripping furniture. Under the Pros column for being a college teacher I write: "Loads of free time; I can refurbish a couple of cabinets on the side." On the other hand, I recall that an old neighbour quit teaching because of department politics. Under the Cons heading, I write: "Have to back-scratch and turn into a 'yes-man' to survive." At the end of the exercise, the only thing I'm trying to decide is whether free afternoons are worth having to butter up an egomaniac faculty head. Not being able to resolve that little dilemma, I move on to writing the pluses and minuses of my other idea – running my own business.

At the top of my Pros column: "No idiot boss. Control over my life." But I know business owners who work long hours, seven days a week, so under my Cons list, I write: "No free time, no vacations. Cabinets won't get restored." Two hours of this and the only decision I can make is that I can't decide. Instead of moving forward, I just keep spinning on the merry-go-round of possibilities.

If you have a list of options and each one is feasible and holds appeal, then there are only two courses of action to follow. The first is to block out a number of weeks to investigate each opportunity fully. This means conducting solid research. Failing that, the second option is to choose the opportunity that is good enough. Throw out the pros and cons list. Instead, write down what you like to do and your basic requirements for income, day-to-day work, home life, leisure time, and personal growth. Consider this list as your line in the sand – what you need for quality of life. Measure your options against this list. If all the choices meet your criteria, then toss a coin. It really doesn't make a whole lot of difference what you select, because you will adapt, you'll make the best of it, and you'll experience some highs and some lows in whatever you do.

My client Gabriel looked at me as if I were a sandwich short of a picnic when I told him this. "Let me get this straight," he said. "You're telling me that it's six of one and a half-dozen of the other whether I join the not-for-profit development agency or stay where I am?"

"You say both meet your non-negotiable criteria. So the question becomes, 'At this juncture in your life, are you more energized by the idea of change or of continuity?'"

Gabriel shrugged and picked up a coin. "Heads, I stay. Tails, I join the not-for-profit," he said.

It came down tails. "Without stopping to think," I asked, "how do you feel now that you're joining the not-for-profit?"

"I'm excited." He took a deep breath. "I like the challenge of a change." He waited two beats. "Then again, what if . . . ?" he started.

"*What if* applies to any choice you make. You can never know the future, so there can only be one answer: if things don't work for you, you'll deal with it."

"That's true," agreed Gabriel. "If I end up not liking the new job, I can always look for another one."

Three months later, Gabriel liked his new job and was putting together a proposal for a co-op program between his organization and his former company. "Just to keep my foot in the door there," he confided in me.

All of us recognize at some level that it's an act of courage to make a decision, whereas endless waffling doesn't quite provoke the same stirrings of admiration. That's why obituaries are full of praise for those who dared to take bold actions regardless of outcome, but never hail the dearly beloved indecisive for their lifetime of wavering over many intriguing ideas.

Still, for argument's sake, let's say you make a choice and, as fate would have it, you pick Door Three, which turns out to be the booby trap. You can take consolation in the truism that change begets change. Every choice, good or bad, triggers a chain reaction that can lead to interesting results. Those with the follow-through factor would add that, at the very least, a wrong choice serves up some useful insight for better decision-making in the future.

NOTE TO SELF: As you get ready to make a move of any kind, you may encounter people who will insist on warning you against rash decision-making. These tend to be nervous, twitchy types who agonize over a menu decision as if it's the last meal they'll ever eat. Doesn't matter that they got the waiter's approval and a nod from the strangers at the next table for the chicken, they still spend half the meal wondering if they should have gone with the fish. To those who would have you deliberate options until you're blue in the face, there is only one thing to say: "The only bad choice is no choice."

People with the follow-through factor insist that the most important thing is to take steps to bring *any* meaningful idea to life, and that the idea itself is secondary. Ideas are like tantalizing recipes. They're all enticing to think about, but the only one that will develop your culinary skill, and give you something to talk about that night around the table, is the recipe that you prepare. And it really doesn't matter if that's a curry or a risotto. In any event, once you follow through on one idea, you'll follow through on another. The heart-pumping feeling of being engaged that you crave is only to be experienced in the act of doing. Want proof? Hand a preschooler a box of building blocks. You'll see her become very serious and involved in putting one on top of another. Each time she balances a block, she'll applaud herself madly, overcome by great pride and happiness. Then when the tower is complete, before you can get out your camera, she'll swing at it and knock it down. The tower doesn't hold her interest, the making of it does.

The artists I've interviewed over the years are like preschoolers, and not just because they too are prone to tantrums. No, they've got the same concentrated interest when they're involved in the task. They say they're in the flow and feeling alive when they are recording the music, editing the movie, writing the book. They may be satisfied with the finished product, although often they are their own toughest critics, but in any case, the end result doesn't energize them as much as the making of it did.

Overthinking leads to paralysis by analysis

You can sit in your chair for years thinking about all the things you could be doing. And five years from now, you'll still be sitting there. Those with the follow-through factor warn against the practice of over-thinking, which they say turns your feet into cement. Instead, people who boast of checkmarks against their list of goals say they make things happen by picking an option in their catalogue of possibilities and moving on it. Write a proposal, draft a business plan, get on a committee, send out your resumé, go back to school, start a writing group. There will be trials and tribulations no matter what, but at least you'll be involved in the act of building, and you'll be far more satisfied and wiser for it. And those with the follow-through factor can guarantee that one step always leads to another.

Trevor, a self-trained artist from Montreal, quit an executive position to travel around the world and work on his art. He sold a few paintings here and there but had to return home periodically and bartend for a while to make money for more travel. On one of his trips, he bumped into a woman who happened to mention an art workshop that she'd taken while holidaying at a spa resort. When Trevor returned home, he wrote up a compelling profile on himself that highlighted his world travels in the pursuit of colour, included some slides of his work, and sent this package to about fifty wellness resorts. He landed a short-term contract at a mountain spa retreat, and one job led to another.

If you'd told Trevor, when he was still sitting in his office stressing over a presentation, that he'd make a career of putting on art workshops at gorgeous resorts, he'd have told you that you'd mixed up his tarot cards with someone else's. When Trevor made the decision to change his life, he didn't focus on what might, or might not, happen down the line.

Instead, he looked at his options and weighed these against his list of non-negotiable criteria for his life.

He had his share of ups and downs before he found a way to live off his artistic talent. Often money was an issue, as was loneliness. There were times when he was tempted to pick up his life as it had been, but instead he stayed true to his line in the sand. "Whenever I was at a crossroads, I asked myself what it was that I really wanted to do and the answer was always, 'I want to paint,'" said Trevor. "So that's what I based my choices on. I didn't return to stay in my hometown because, for various reasons, I couldn't manage to crack open my paints there."

Although Trevor is resourceful and multi-talented and has a postgraduate degree, he managed to avoid paralysis from analysis of the many "coulds" and "shoulds" for his life. Like everyone with the follow-through factor, he didn't get caught up in trying to predict his future in fine detail. Instead, he put his focus and energy into something he cared about. That's the only way to free yourself to put one foot in front of the other and do something.

CUE CARD

- When you're at a crossroads and every direction holds your interest, don't waste your life standing at the intersection, trying desperately to determine which path might be the best one. Those who follow through know that "best" doesn't exist.

- There's "good" and "not so good" on every road. It doesn't matter which path you pick, just pick one and start moving. You'll not only adapt to the terrain, you'll leave your mark one way or another. And one step leads to another. But if you don't walk, you're not going to make any footprints, anywhere.

EXERCISE
Making a choice

When you have a lot of great ideas for what you could do, it's that much harder to settle on one and stay focused on making it happen. Keep in mind that you have time in a life to follow through on many ideas – but you need to start somewhere.

Whatever decision you make is better than not making a decision. Those with the follow-through factor confirm that the insights gained from pursuing one option will prove invaluable when the time comes to pursue the next big thing on your list.

The following exercise is designed to help you decide which choice is the right one at this time in your life.

1. *List the choices you are considering.*
2. *Determine your line in the sand. (What is non-negotiable for you? What conditions do you deem essential for quality of life?)*
3. *Which of the choices allow you to stick to your line in the sand? (Which meet your non-negotiable criteria?)*
4. *What are three to five activities that you might do in a day that are particularly interesting to you?*
5. *Which of the choices under consideration would allow you to do all, or most, of these activities?*
6. *What are three to five activities that you dislike doing in the course of the day?*
7. *Which of the choices under consideration allow you to avoid all, or most, of these?*

SEVEN

Yes, but I'm not sure this is my passion

Every self-help book under the sun, every coaching manual, every friend who has imbibed one too many glasses of wine says the same thing: Know your passion. Follow your passion. Live your passion. Breathe your passion. What's with this fixation already?

How many people do you know personally who are truly living and breathing their passion? Pimply adolescents in the throes of first love and golf fanatics don't count. And workaholics don't cut it either. They're not so much passionate as obsessed. So maybe you can name a handful of folk, maybe you can't.

The fact is that passion is as elusive as a waiter in an airport bar, yet most of us think we can't possibly follow through without it. The number-one reason people drop projects is because, after the initial flirtation, they find the work doesn't thrill them as much as they imagined it would. Like a disappointing third date, the spark turned out to be an illusion.

I've heard it from hundreds – if they could only find something to do that they were truly, madly passionate about they'd follow through to the moon. But hey, they just haven't found their soul-idea. Tell that to someone who has the follow-through factor and they'll brush you off as a romantic fool.

Does this mean the tenacious are cold fish? Not at all, but they are realists. Like most of us, they're very much interested in uncovering their true passion. They, too, attend workshops to find their life purpose and are excited to realize that Lithuanian folk dancing or baking artisanal bread electrifies them. But the difference between those who follow through and the rest of the world is that people who persevere don't expect that opening a dance school or bread shop is going to be an earth-moving experience. They accept that it's going to be a lot of hard work and hassles.

No matter how hot and excited you were when you sat at the bar and sketched out your latest idea on a cocktail napkin, you'll feel the sting of a cold shower once you get into the nuts and bolts of your plan. But nowadays, passion is the new fibre. We're told we've got to have a daily dose for a happy, fulfilled life. So we figure if we're not feeling the love 24/7, whatever we're doing can't be the right thing.

What exactly is this must-have emotion of the decade, and where do you buy it? I plumbed the historical definition of the word for clues. I learned that "passion" derives from the Latin *passio*, a word that originated in the second century to describe the supreme ecstatic suffering of Jesus in relation to the Crucifixion. Over coffee with a Jesuit priest, I asked how anyone could expect to experience passion in regard to, say, running a focus group or manufacturing anti-sweat wear for women with hot flashes. He wasn't sure and advised me to turn to the arts for a more earthly interpretation of the emotion.

Writers, filmmakers, composers, and painters have always had a lot to say on the subject. But surprisingly, they don't veer far from the original spirit of the word. The message in their work boils down to this: passion is equal parts exhilaration and agony. Like the perfect love that can never be, passion is both transcendent joy and sublime pain. It's a spectacular firework, an explosion of energy and beauty that overwhelms and then just as quickly fades to black.

Don't expect all passion, all the time

Passion is the tsunami of all feeling. It comes over you, retreats, and leaves you gasping. But a key characteristic of passion is that it doesn't hang around for the duration. And thank God, really. If you've ever been swept away by a passionate love affair or had the bad luck to find yourself trapped on a plane next to someone who is crazy in love and can speak of nothing else, you know how all-consuming it is.

When in the clutches of passion, you can't eat, you can't sleep, you can't think or talk of anything else. You certainly have a tough time remembering to pick up the dry-cleaning and a glue gun for little Johnny's Grade 2 project. Eventually, to the great relief of your bored-silly friends, your love affair either dies out or turns into something more manageable and less obsessive that allows you to get on with the job of everyday living. Even the poet Lord Byron, adored since the early 1800s for his exquisite romantic sensibility, had to admit: "There is no such thing as a life of passion any more than a continuous earthquake, or an eternal fever."

It's the curse of the follow-through-challenged to question their "true passion." You find yourself taking a few steps in one direction and then fretting that maybe there's something far more soul-satisfying out there for you to do. Soon enough, you hit upon a radically new notion to play with, one that's typically unrelated to your area of experience. Progress on your original plan screeches to a halt as you fall in love with your latest idea, which is usually undeveloped and far-fetched. Meanwhile, the years go by and all you have to show for your brushes with passion is a wastebasket full of crumpled napkins.

By its very nature, passion is not sustainable, so why is it that, since the rise of the self-development movement, we've all been on a mad quest to not only get the feeling but keep it burning like an eternal flame in our bellies? Probably because we've been directed to adopt some mighty rare exceptions as our role models.

I've interviewed dozens of people who truly do live a passionate life, day in, day out. They are deeply in love with their occupation, and they make no distinction between what they do and who they are. These are the principal ballet dancers, the Tour de France cyclists, the orchestral composers, the mountain climbers, the brilliant and driven activists, philanthropists, and entrepreneurs. True to their passion, they live on a roller coaster, careening between mental or physical angst and unimaginable highs. They're always determined to go faster, farther, higher on the next ride. But by their own admission, their single focus on their performance doesn't leave much time or interest for anything else, like getting home for dinner by six in the evening. They say they pay a price for being so intense, but they just couldn't imagine living any other way.

These are not ordinary people living extraordinary lives. These are born visionaries whom many scientists believe are genetically programmed for a life of dedication and fervor. We can admire them, but those of us who aren't extremists and who don't have single-track minds can't very well expect to be just like them.

Average people who follow through don't get hooked on thinking of their project as their big fat passion. They don't demand that every day be a "wow" day. Those with the follow-through factor don't even toss the word *passion* around. Instead, they say they're "really interested" or "intrigued" by their project, and they think it would be "fun" to see it through to completion. These ordinary people with grit will tell you that you can definitely manage to pursue an interest in between picking up groceries, balancing a chequebook and paying attention to family, friends, and dogs.

The prevailing belief that you must be totally "passionate" about your idea or project is unrealistic, not to mention downright demotivating. When you set the bar so unattainably high, you just set yourself up for disappointment.

The client who couldn't commit

"You know," my client Ron confessed, staring out my office window, "I'm not sure being in charge of sponsorships will be all that."

"All that what?" I wondered.

He shook his head, impatiently. "All *that*."

Ron worked in the public affairs division of a large manufacturer. For months he had been working energetically to get his company to set up a sponsorship division. He had been pumped about the different events his company could sponsor, and the innovative ways he could market his firm's involvement. The CEO had finally approved Ron's proposal, but now his enthusiasm was starting to wane. I could read the signs. Ron was falling out of love . . . again.

"Do I really want to devote all my time and energy to the logistical headaches of sponsorship? There's so much red tape and petty politics. You know, I was thinking I'd prefer to work directly with the artists."

"You mean have your company sponsor the artist, not the festival?"

"No, that wouldn't work. I was thinking I'd like to be an agent, or maybe a promoter."

"And you figure agents and promoters don't have logisti-cal hassles to deal with?" I asked incredulously. Didn't every-body know about Mariah Carey's long list of impossible demands when she tours?

"I'm not saying it would be easier, but I'd be more into the work, you know. I'd care more."

Skepticism is admittedly not an attractive quality, but I had to admit to it. "Ron, just two weeks ago you said you really cared about helping keep cultural festivals and events viable through corporate sponsorship."

He came back at me with "but" after "but," and not one of them was convincing.

If Ron made passion his prerequisite for moving ahead, he'd find himself doing what so many do, treading water while waiting to be overcome by something so irresistible and wonderful that he would be compelled to go for it, no matter what. It would be a long, long wait, punctuated by a lot of false starts. In Ron's case, he could find that while he might not be "passionate" about some aspects of sponsor-ship, he might equally dislike some parts of an agent's work.

Even the most glamorous occupation is a yin and yang of interesting and not so enjoyable activities. People who doubt that have never interviewed exhausted actors and musicians on multi-city promotional tours, watched high-profile devel-opers wade through mind-numbing zoning issues, or heard magazine writers curse their editors for demanding yet another rewrite of their piece.

87

So, do you have to give up on the idea of passion? Compare it to a relationship. Do you partner with an interesting, fun person who leaves the last shrimp on the plate for you, or do you sit around and dream about someone with a fascinating lifestyle, a huge bank account, and a perfect physique sweeping you off your feet in a movie-style romance? Some would say, don't bother dressing up for anyone but that brown-eyed, chiselled babe with big bucks. Those people tend to spend a lot of their years hanging around in their bathrobes, going nowhere. People with the follow-through factor go out for Chinese, order the shrimp, and make some memories.

So, passion-seekers, stop jumping from idea to idea long enough to listen up. Don't worry if you're not bursting with enthusiasm every time you interact with your idea. No one else out there is experiencing perma-passion. Some days you love the thing you do, and some days you're really not all that sure about it. Some aspects of your project are a blast, other aspects gives you a headache. A project is like a person: it has good and bad points. No one and nothing is perfect.

Your project doesn't have to be remarkable for you to consider it worth your while. If, overall, it stimulates you, involves activities you mostly enjoy, and gives you a chance to stretch and learn, then it's the right plan for right now.

NOTE TO SELF: It's child's play to punch holes in an ambition and come up with a list of reasons why an idea is not worthy of your interest. You want to climb Mount Everest? Oh please, do something more original than hike that old trash heap. You want to write a book? The bookstores are full of books nobody buys. Put energy into something that pays. You want to go into sales? And spend your life chasing clients? I don't think so. Do something where people come to you. You want to be a psychologist? What, and listen to people whine all day? Are you nuts? Do something fun with your life. For many of us, it's almost second nature to act as a human jackhammer and find cracks in a plan to bring it down. The best way to unplug those internal, and external, jackhammers is to agree with the negative assertions that are valid without buying into doom-and-gloom conclusions. It's true, more and more people are attempting Everest. It must be amazing, or why would people pay huge bucks to try it? For sure, most authors don't make money, so they have to be getting something else out of writing. It's undeniable that psychologists deal with people who are upset. It must be stimulating to help them gain a new perspective.

Stick with your current project through thick and thin and a funny thing will happen – you'll grow more attached to it. Think of a project as a thousand-piece jigsaw puzzle. It's exciting to start, but so tedious to continue at times. And yet, every time you match two pieces of the puzzle together, you get a little spark that drives you to keep going until it's completed. The more you do, the more you want to do.

Perseverance fuels interest. A medieval history professor told me she persevered with her studies because she knew that the more she learned about her subject, the more her interest and attachment to it would grow.

Typically, as soon as passion-seekers decide to commit to a project, they become haunted by the question "Is this all there is for me?" There's no cause to panic; committing to a particular project doesn't mean you'll never do anything else in your life. Those with the follow-through factor will tell you this is only one of many ideas you'll take from start to finish. You can be sure that the more experience you have in following through on a plan, the more plans you'll develop and complete in the years ahead.

Your project is one interesting chapter in your life story. Follow it through and it will take you to the next chapter.

CUE CARD

- Don't let a lack of ongoing passion stop you cold. Passion is a surge of intense emotion, not an everyday feeling. No one feels the love 24/7 when developing an idea and struggling to make it work.
- Substitute the word *interest* for the word *passion*, and follow through with your plan.
- You'll find when you stick with something through thick and thin, setback and success, your affection for it actually grows, not diminishes.

EIGHT

Yes, but I don't have a clue how to proceed

I know and you know that you're flying by the seat of your pants right now. Congratulations, that takes moxie. You're doing something new, something you've never done before, so naturally you can't be sure you're doing everything, or anything, right. It would be nice if you had a clue, but failing that, what are you going to do but fake it until you make it?

"Fake it until you make it" is a frequent refrain of those who have the follow-through factor. It's a good idea to tack their motto over your desk and on your bathroom mirror. It may well be the only navigational tool you have right now. Obviously, it's nowhere near as good a guide as experience, but since you're a little short of experience at the moment, faking it is the next best thing. Does it work? Without fail, just not always as quickly as you'd like. But you can take comfort in this other handy little maxim: "Better late than never."

Everyone who sets out on a new path comes to a point, usually sooner rather than later, where they realize they don't actually know which foot should go in front of the other. A lot of people get so stumped that they don't move forward at all. Those who follow through just make an executive decision. There's only ever one way to proceed when you're unsure of how to move ahead, and that's to close your eyes and jump.

Meet Jack. He had been working in the marketing department of a paint company for a few years when he decided he wanted to become a colour consultant instead. At the time, no one really knew what that was and, frankly, neither did Jack. He just figured he'd go to people's houses and, for a price, advise them which colour to paint their living room. It made perfect sense to him; people spend a fortune buying sea moss paint only to sit down twelve hours later, look around the room, and wail that they've painted themselves into a can of creamed spinach. They'd save themselves a lot of money and stress by having someone warn them that sea moss is the wrong backdrop for a paisley couch.

In truth, Jack's resumé didn't exactly scream "colour expert." The only experience he could draw on were his years, prior to college, as a sales clerk at a high-end department store. The manager of men's wear used to praise him for his way with people and his fashion sense. Jack could turn guys who arrived wearing their belts under their armpits into hip, colour-coordinated fashionistas.

Long story short, Jack's company reviewed his credentials and said there was no way it would go out on a limb and position him as its trustworthy residential colour consultant. As a small consolation, the company said Jack was free to develop his business independently, after hours. And like any contractor, he could get the standard ten percent discount on paints purchased for clients. Without the paint company promoting his services, Jack was clueless as to how to begin to grow his consultancy. So he did the first thing everybody does: he focused on getting business cards made. Designing them took him weeks. When at last he picked up his box of cards from the printer, he panicked. Now what?

Often people with a new idea and no map for how to proceed put their energy into reading books and surfing the Internet for information. Months and months whiz by while they overload on research. Sadly, at some point, you do have to leave the safety of the computer cocoon and take your idea out into the world.

Jack had done his research. Ask him anything about complementary hues and the effects of sunlight or fluorescent and sixty-watt light on colour, and he had an answer for you. After working his way through books on colour, he moved on to the business self-help section. In time he found a template for a business plan and completed it. His plan written, he panicked again.

Then he closed his eyes and jumped. With his heart in his throat, he forced himself to contact five interior designers. In his business plan, he had pegged interior design consultants as possible allies. Jack relayed how a typical call went.

"Hi, I'd like to let you know about a service that I'm offering that can help you and your clients," he'd begin.

"What are you selling?" barked back the interior designer.

"I'm a colour consultant and . . ."

"You work with hair? You've got the wrong number."

"No, I help people figure out the best colours for their homes, to match their furniture, their personalities . . ."

"I'm an interior designer. That's part of my job. Why in the world would I send people to you?"

"Right, then. Well, thanks for your time."

"So what did you learn from that exercise?" I asked Jack.

"That I won't be getting any clients from interior designers. And to specify that I don't do highlights."

Next, Jack tackled furniture stores, since he had included those in his business plan as well. Jack would ask the store manager if he could leave his business cards and usually got a discouraging reply. Apparently, customers weren't in the habit of asking for colour consultants, and managers didn't feel it was their job to prod them to do so.

Eventually, through trial and error, Jack did build a business. It got its launch by word of mouth after he helped friends of friends choose colours for their new homes. Bolstered by his portfolio of before-and-after shots and letters from satisfied clients, he approached his company again. This time, they agreed to let him display his business card at the cash counter at all city paint stores. This wasn't quite the all-out company endorsement that Jack had been dreaming of, but it was better than nothing. Jack spent a lot of time at these paint stores talking to managers and putting on in-store presentations. Now he's a full-time colour consultant.

Jack's tale of risk and rejection is the same for just about anyone following through in an arena that is new to them. At some point, no matter what your project is, you're going to have to sell the idea to someone. And that's never easy when you're a newbie. The best you can do is practise your pitch on a C-list of prospects. Perfecting your sales spiel is a matter of trial and error, and it's wise to make your mistakes with those who are unlikely or unprofitable prospects. When you've learned from your errors, move to your B-list before tackling your A-list of best prospects.

Pitching a product or service is always a piece of cake when you couldn't care less about the outcome, but it's terri-fying when you feel you have a lot at stake. The majority of us look to friends and family for counsel. This can be help-ful, so long as you don't confuse feedback with informed, expert advice.

When it comes to taking a leap, you've only got yourself to trust

95

David Chilton, author of *The Wealthy Barber,* is a legend among self-publishers for selling millions of copies of his self-published book. His guide to financial planning remains in high demand more than ten years after he brought it to market. But when he picked up those first boxes of books from the printers, he had no prior experience to guide his next move. However, while he was writing his book, he distributed finished chapters to friends and family to gauge their reaction. David said he didn't turn to his pals just for a cursory show of support; he genuinely wanted to learn if people found the chapters engaging and helpful. Their positive feedback proved to be a great boost of confidence that helped him persevere through the early, uncertain days of figuring out how to promote the book. David sought feedback on the book's content, but he didn't rely on those with no experience in self-publishing or marketing for step-by-step direction on how to promote his book.

Use friends and colleagues as fact-checkers, sounding boards, and cheerleaders. But don't make them into advisers in areas they know even less about than you do. When it comes to making actual decisions, resign yourself to the fact that you're on your own. As much as possible, seek advice from people in the know. Otherwise, make an executive decision. But don't let the peanut gallery determine your next step. It never feels good to discover you made a wrong choice, but it feels much worse to realize that you blew an opportunity because you followed the advice of Mr. Beaton from the next office who, now that you think about it, has the business sense of a pea.

My client Nicky wanted to become a children's book illustrator but couldn't decide which samples of her work would impress publishers and land her an assignment. She worried that she'd blow her chances if she submitted the wrong drawings. So she did the natural thing: she sought the advice of everyone and their gerbil, and received dozens of conflicting opinions. When, after much agonizing, she finally made a decision, her best friend insisted she would be better off creating an entirely new series of drawings from scratch. At this point, Nicky became so discouraged that she was ready to toss her ambition, along with her drawings, into the garbage.

What were the credentials of this friend who was adamant that Nicky's choices were wrong? Nicky described her as "super smart and extremely successful." She did have an awesome track record, but in investment analysis, not book publishing. She never spent time with kids and, when asked if she knew the book *Goodnight Moon* (a children's classic), she said that she avoided apocalyptic stories. She may know how to read a stock ticker better than most, but Nicky had absolutely no reason to abide by her opinions about her work.

NOTE TO SELF: Everyone wants to be an expert. Ask someone for advice and they'll give it to you, whether or not they're qualified, because no one is going to pass up a chance to pontificate. An added perk for advisers is that they figure they're absolved from responsibility, thanks to this little disclaimer that they always toss in at the end: "But don't listen to me. What do I know? You have to decide for yourself." Terrific. So all that babbling was just a waste of fifteen minutes of your life. When you're already feeling uncertain, the last thing you need is to be confused by even more inexpert and less thoughtful points of views than your own. So if you're going to ask non-experts for direction, stick to specific queries about one aspect of your project. For example, Nicky stopped asking friends which pictures she should include in her portfolio and instead asked them to choose between two sketches of koalas.

Sometimes ignorance can be bliss

A lack of knowledge can be a blessing. It frees you up to try things you wouldn't attempt if you knew better. When I decided I wanted to expand my business to include coaching, I shopped a free lunch-and-learn presentation to any company that would bite. Now I look back at those first brown-bag seminars and cringe. I packed in too much detailed information that nobody cared about, and I raced through too many activities in the hour, forcing people to speed-talk with their mouth full of tuna salad sandwich. But there are times in life when it's helpful to be a little naive. It was a good thing that

I believed I was adept at offering introductory seminars on coaching, or I'd never have got up the nerve to strut my stuff in boardrooms. Thanks to my unfounded confidence that came from not knowing any better, I acquired the experience I needed. It didn't take me long to refine my lunch-and-learn and I did land a terrific contract.

Not being sure of how best to pitch your idea or take your plan to the next stage is a common problem. It's maddening that you have to go through the pain and sometimes outright humiliation of screwing up before getting wise to a better way. But rest assured that these inevitable missteps will end up as great battle stories that you'll use to inspire first-time bumblers who follow behind you.

Everyone who has followed through in a new arena has reams of school-of-hard-knocks tales to tell. And it's these chronicles of dumb moves and despair on the way to getting what we want that make us so interesting to ourselves and others. Not to mention that these wince-worthy stories are valuable to keep in your back pocket for when you need to liven up a dinner party.

Worse than a shaky start is not getting out the door at all because you don't know how. It's common for people to give up their great idea because they're clueless as to how to implement it. But nowadays, courtesy of Google, it's usually fairly easy to find out the information you need to take the first steps. And at least we can all claim some experience with research. At one time or another, we managed to figure out for ourselves how to get a job or shop for a house, secure a mortgage, sell a car, get a divorce, choose a pet, move to a new city. When you think about it, there have probably been dozens of occasions over the years when you started off in the dark and somehow stumbled into the light.

Answers are born from questions

Those with the follow-through factor will tell you that you don't have to know nearly as much as you may think when you set out in pursuit of your goal. It's a learn-as-you-go process, and all you need to do to move ahead is focus on your very next step. When you're unsure what that step should be, resort to the question that has launched a thousand success stories: "What do I need to find out first?"

The "ask and you shall receive" principle really does work wonders. Let's say you want to import baskets from Nigeria, but you've never imported anything before other than two bottles of rum from your last Caribbean vacation. So you ask yourself, "Where can I get information about importing goods?" A little Googling will put you in the loop and alert you to courses on how to import. Knowledge builds on knowledge. After acquiring preliminary information, you will be ready to identify and query people in the know. And presto, you will receive some answers. Next, you test the process again, this time asking, "Where can I find distributors for these baskets?" Sure enough, the question prompts more research, which leads to more insight. It doesn't matter what your goal is; figuring out how to make it happen starts with breaking down your idea into questions.

I've found that the journalist's standard five W (and one H) questions are reliable launching pads whether you want to start a new business, suggest a new service in the workplace, or develop a personal interest: what, who, why, where, when, and how.

Here's how these questions propelled two clients to move ahead on their ambitions. Jasmine, a purchasing agent, envisioned a get-away retreat for moms and toddlers. Anderson, a systems analyst, wanted to learn the craft of stained glass.

1. What?

Jasmine asked herself, "What activities will I offer?" She found her answer by reading a lot of parenting magazines, as well as talking to public health nurses and new mothers.

Anderson asked himself what kind of art he wanted to create.

2. Who?

Jasmine investigated who would likely comprise her largest market. She discussed her idea with members of associations, travel agents, first-time moms, single moms, moms of toddlers, moms of older children, etc.

Anderson asked himself who in the market could help him learn a new craft.

3. Why?

Jasmine researched all the reasons why moms would be, and wouldn't be, interested in her offering so she could hype the positives and address the negatives.

Anderson asked himself why working with stained glass was the right medium for him.

4. Where?

To answer her question "Where would I hold the retreat and how much would it cost?" Jasmine called nearby inns and bed-and-breakfasts.

Anderson asked himself where he would find a place to create his artwork, and investigated the possibility of converting his basement into a workshop.

5. When?

Jasmine talked to inns and moms about optimal times for a weekend retreat.

Anderson found out when instructional workshops were offered.

6. How?

As a result of asking herself how she would reach her market, Jasmine did an Internet search for organizations and publications for new parents that she could contact to promote her retreat.

Anderson asked himself how he would need to rearrange his schedule to fit in weekly classes.

When thinking about offering a new service or product of any kind, the answer to the question "How do I contact my market?" typically starts with a lot of tedious writing of plans, proposals, and promotional materials and ends with your knocking on doors, acting as if you know what you're doing.

"Act as if" is a standard coaching instruction that can work miracles for you. Of course, it's not that easy when you're quaking inside, convinced that the rest of the world can see through your inexperience. But it helps to remind yourself that people see only what you show them. And it's not fair to show your fears about your competency to potential clients and make your insecurity their problem.

Whether you are experienced or new to the field, your job is to reassure people that you will deliver what you say you will. Your challenge is to figure out how to acquire the necessary information and/or skills to meet expectations. Your audience doesn't need or care to know about these behind-the-scenes logistics. When you're sitting in a plane, you don't really want your pilot announcing, "We'll be flying at an altitude of thirty-five thousand feet and, by the way, folks, this is my first flight sitting in the captain's chair so I'm feeling kind of nervous and having some heart palpitations. But you all just relax and enjoy the flight. I'm hoping everything will turn out fine."

Naturally, people who are tackling a project for the first time or starting out in a new business feel they don't know as much as they could. However, as a newbie, you may offer extraordinary value to your team or client. No one works harder than those who need to come off as more experienced than they feel.

Jack, the colour consultant, still recalls how he couldn't eat or sleep for days before his meeting with his first paying clients. He was convinced that they would see him as the imposter he felt himself to be. "I remember lying awake at night, wondering how I could be such a moron as to think that I could pull off what schooled, experienced interior designers do."

Jack said that what helped him "bluff" his way through his first paid consultations was to remind himself of an anecdote he'd heard about a couple who were dissatisfied with the work of an established, and expensive, interior designer. "I got a lot of comfort from knowing that even big names can mess up. I kept telling myself, 'Well, the client may not like my ideas, but then there's no guarantee that they'd like the ideas of a better-known consultant either.'" Experience doesn't automatically equal brilliance. That said, Jack admitted that he put in a lot of unpaid hours during those first assignments, which he didn't begrudge because he felt he was learning on the job.

Act as if you've got a clue, even when you don't

When you act as if you know what you're doing, you move ahead with strength, in the best way you can think of at the time. But for those who flunked Shakespeare, how exactly do you learn to "act as if"? William James, the influential

American psychologist and philosopher of the early 1900s, came up with the strategy that people continue to use today. He insisted that our physical actions provoke our feelings. Smile, he said, and you'll feel happier. Sob, and you'll feel sad. He wrote in his essay *The Gospel of Relaxation,* "The voluntary path to cheerfulness, if our spontaneous cheerfulness be lost, is to sit up cheerfully, to look round cheerfully, and to act and speak as if cheerfulness were already there. If such conduct does not make you soon feel cheerful, nothing else on that occasion can. So to feel brave, act as if we *were* brave, use all our will to that end, and a courage-fit will very likely replace the fit of fear."

Psychologist Paul Ekman, a world pioneer in non-verbal communications, has conducted extensive research that supports James's theory. In a dialogue with the Dalai Lama, recorded in the book *Destructive Emotions: How We Can Overcome Them,* Ekman expands on the link between facial expression and changes in the brain. He notes, "The face is not simply a means of display, but also a means of activating emotion." Just as James insisted, science confirms that the very act of smiling, regardless of how you actually feel, causes brain activity that is typically associated with good feelings. And frowning is shown to cause brain activity typically associated with sadness. In other words, puff out your chest and strut, and you'll start to actually feel more confident. If it seems like a tall order, remember you have a choice. You can decide to allow your audience to see and hear your uncertainty or timidity, or you can opt to project the strength that comes from knowing, somehow or another, you'll deliver on what you promise.

"Fake it until you make it" means you proceed with an assuredness founded not on experience but on faith in your ability to problem-solve. It means that though you might not know if you are going about things in the best possible way, you keep on going regardless, and you pretend to the world that you're confident you're on the right track. And you stay on that track until you have good reason to try another tack. And then you try again, a bit wiser. That's what everyone who follows through does, and that's no bluff.

CUE CARD

- Since you're trying something new, you can't be expected to have the answers you need. But you won't find all the expertise you wish you had in books or from friends who don't know any more than you do.
- You don't need to know as much as you think to begin following through on your goal – it's a learn-as-you-go process. Break your idea down into questions and take it one question at a time.
- At some point, you may have to be prepared to "fake it until you make it." Act as if you do have a clue and boldly follow your plan, despite not being certain that you're doing it right. Only trial and error will give you the experience you lack today.

How to "act as if" in three steps

To fake it until you make it you often need to work at appearing more self-assured than you might be feeling. Remember, people see only what you show them. Whether you are experienced or new to the field, your job is to reassure people that you will deliver what you say you will.

Here's a terrific three-step strategy to help you act as if you have all the confidence in the world to put those you want to impress at ease. Most important, *when you act like the person you want to be, you become the person you want to be.*

Step 1: Is that me or a mouse talking?
Typically, we show our nervousness through our facial expressions, voice, and posture. Some of us walk into meetings and talk too fast, others among us mumble, twitch in our seats, or keep our eyes downcast. I had a client who, when anxious, would repeatedly scratch the back of his head, undoubtedly distracting the table with worries of lice.

The way to stop yourself from sending out distress signals is to enter any interaction with a very strong image in your head of how you *don't* want to appear and how you *do*. This technique is a form of bio-feedback — you remain aware of projecting traits you don't like so that you can self-correct.

Picture a character, real or fictional, who is timid and nervous. It could be a person or an animal, such as a mouse or rabbit. Write down who or what you are imagining:

_____

Now imagine that just before you enter a meeting or a new work environment, you are given the personality of this person/animal. Answer these questions:

How do you feel as this person or animal?

_____
_____
_____

What is your posture? How are you holding yourself?

_____
_____
_____

What is your facial expression? What attitude are you conveying?

_____
_____
_____

Where are you looking when you speak ? _____

_____
_____

What is your voice like? Too high or fast, too slow, too low?

_____

_____

_____

What impression are you making on those you wish to persuade? _____

_____

_____

Do you believe you will leave people feeling confident that you can deliver what you say you can? _____

_____

_____

Step 2: The eagle has landed

Now imagine a very powerful person or animal. Write down who or what you are imagining:

_____

Your goal is to enter a meeting or workplace with the confidence and power of this person or animal. Answer these questions:

How do you feel as this person or animal?

_____

_____

_____

What is your posture? How are you holding yourself?

_____

_____

_____

What is your facial expression? What attitude are you conveying?

_____

_____

_____

Where are you looking when you speak ? _____

_____

_____

What is your voice like?

_____

_____

_____

What impression are you making on those you wish to persuade? _____

_____

_____

Do you believe you will leave people feeling confident that you can deliver what you say you can? _____

_____

_____

_____

Step 3: Remembering to "act as if"

Find a touchstone that brings to mind the powerful person/animal you pictured above. It may be a picture or perhaps an object such as a pen or watch, or a stone that represents strength.

Look at the picture or touch the object to help remind yourself to adopt the desired physical and mental attitudes of self-confidence.

If, during an interaction with one or more people, you still find yourself overcome by insecurity, ask yourself whether you want to come across as the nervous person you described above or the powerful one. You'll discover that just asking yourself the question will automatically prompt you to adjust your behaviour.

NINE

Yes, but I'm afraid

F ear has a funny face. Look in the mirror, make your eyes go wide, and frown. Hello, you are looking at fear – and it's looking right back at you like a bug-eyed emu caught in the headlights of life.

With just the slightest bit of encouragement, fear will move in and take over your mind like an unwanted house guest from hell. And when fear's in the house, self-trust moves out. So when people tell you not to worry because most things we fret about never come to pass – and even if the worst should happen, you'll learn to cope – you're not reassured. Instead, you freak. You rush to the washroom to splash water on your face and catch sight of a bug-eyed emu in the mirror staring out at you. And at that moment, the last few dregs of confidence in yourself go down the drain.

We all listen to our fears. It's human nature to do so. Fear is a survival instinct. Without it, humans probably wouldn't be around and the ants would have inherited the earth. If we hadn't retreated to the cave in fright when we heard the roar of sabre-toothed tigers, we would have evolved no further than dinner for big cats. To this very day, we can thank the jitters for reminding us to avoid dark alleyways and to stand clear of novice golfers. So, of course, we consider fear our protector. The problem is fear can be a bit of a control freak. Our instinct for self-preservation is so keen that, left unchecked, it turns into a crossing guard carried away with road safety. Put one foot on the road and he's blowing his whistle for you to stop right now – there's a car fifteen blocks away. At this rate, how will you get to where you need to go? You won't.

Fear keeps you right where you are. If you try to push it aside, it'll fight back. And fear fights dirty. It can land a punch right in your stomach. You may be standing at a podium, in no physical danger whatsoever, but fear is tormenting your body like a schoolyard bully. Your audience could be composed of the nicest people in the world, say an auditorium full of nuns or folksingers, and yet your gut is in a knot, your heart is racing, your palms are sweating, your knees are shaking. Why? Do you think one of the nuns is going to sneak in a karate chop when you least suspect it? No, it's your fear being overprotective. It's saying, "Get out of there, you goof. There's a chance you'll bomb, so back away slowly from the podium."

Fear is nothing if not manipulative. If you stand up to its physical bullying, it'll quickly change tactics and take on

113

the guise of a cliché-quoting wise crone to remind you, "The trodden path is the safest." Argue for taking a chance, and fear turns up the heat. If you're going to insist on taking a risk, fear is going to have to get nasty. For your own good, it'll tell you loud and clear that you're not made of the right stuff. "Hold it, pal," it may say. "Those who rule in the jungle are lions, and you, my friend, are more meerkat than wild cat!"

Fear is a wimp in disguise

Fear is excessively risk-averse, which is why it likes you to stick with the status quo and not move out of your safe little wading pool into the great big blue. Maybe life isn't ideal in your turtle-shaped plastic pool, but at least there's nothing scarier in there than a couple of drowned flies. As the fearful always say, "The devil you know is better than the one you don't." In fact, there's a fifty–fifty chance that the unknown devil is the more pleasant of the two, but you would have to roll the dice to find out. And why risk it? From the perspective of fear, life is a fragile house of cards. Jostle any one of those cards and the whole thing can come crashing down. This fate could be so easily avoided if you would just leave everything the way it is. Don't mess with stuff.

Working in cahoots with fear is your inner critic. If your inner critic were a full-fledged person, you'd want to run from him after spending two minutes in his company. This judgmental chatterbox that lives inside every one of us feeds on our insecurities and delights in reminding us of our shortcomings. Every time you felt that you'd let some- one down, be it a parent or a Grade 6 teacher, your inner critic took note. Every time someone sighed that they had expected more of you, the inner critic registered the com- plaint. Every time you messed up at something, the inner critic stored the info. Every time you felt you didn't meas- ure up to someone's standards – be those the standards of people you know or those set by society at large – the inner critic was there, jotting down your feelings of inadequacy to remind you about them later.

So in one ear you've got the fear instinct urging you to lie low because it's a dangerous world out there, where bad things happen to well-intentioned people. People lose their jobs, their dates, their cats, all the time. If all is okay in your life, then for God's sake, do not touch your house of cards. Again and again, your fear instinct blows its whistle to beg you to stay on the curb and not to tempt fate. And in the other ear, you've got the inner critic reeling off all your flaws and asking how, with your deficiencies and your track record of failure, can you expect to shake up your world and succeed?

It's tempting to view our fear and our inner critic as lov- ing parts of ourselves that just want us to take care. But these are not the murmurings of the nurturing inner grandma who urges us to wear a coat in case it turns cold out there. Fear and self-criticism are paralyzing forces that, if left to run the show, would prevent us from going out to play at all. The voice of care encourages action but reminds us to proceed with our eyes open. When we tell ourselves to be careful, we're activating our radar. When we tell ourselves that we aren't good enough to pull off our ambition, and we'll face disastrous consequences if we try, we're shutting ourselves down.

Fear and its evil twin, the inner critic, are facts of life. A small minority of people, such as those who swim with sharks or ice climb, must have been in the washroom when the gods were handing out fear and self-doubt, but everyone else got their fair share. People with the follow-through factor don't feel more confident or safer than anyone else, but they learn to become like those new skaters you see wobbling into the middle of the ice rink. Despite their knock knees, they're determined to move away from the wall and join the fast-moving circle of seasoned skaters. They feel twinges of concern, but they're absolutely determined to enjoy themselves anyway. Fear always wants to come along for the ride, so all you can do is tune it out.

NOTE TO SELF: Anytime someone thinks about doing something new that has a degree of risk involved, people start playing the dreaded game of "What will you do if . . . ?" Here's how it goes. You mention that you're going to quit a job and go into business for yourself. "What will you do if you get sick? What will happen to your business?" Let's say you have an easy answer to that one. "I'll take out insurance." Your opponent will counter, "What will you do if you can't afford insurance?" You answer something about looking for a job again, if you have to. "But you'll be that much older. What will you do if you're too old to get hired? Anyway, what if you're sick? You can't work if you're sick." You mention you could sell the house if necessary. "But your house is your only security. What will you do?" The object of this popular game is to make fear win and you lose. Most of us can go several rounds before we capitulate. We may have a good Plan A, a not-so-awful Plan B, and a tolerable Plan C up our sleeve, but our Plan D looks pretty bad, even to us. And anyway, who can come up with a satisfactory answer to "What if an earthquake hits?" The rotten truth is that there's no way to win this game, so the best thing is not to play. "I'll jump off that bridge when I get to it" is as good an answer as any. Things could go wrong, things could work out great. No one has a crystal ball, but the good news is that no matter what happens, we almost always manage much better than we thought we would.

Fear has its valid points. But for every scary "What if?" you could argue, "So what?" Maya, who started her own ad agency targeting Indian and South Asian consumers living in North America, recognized that the only answer to the question "What if your agency doesn't prove profitable over time?" was "So what?" She said that if, after a couple of years, her business failed to make money, she would look for a job with an established agency. And what if nobody hired her? That's an unlikely scenario, but if it came to pass, Maya said she'd pursue contract work. She's a resourceful person; she would do *something*.

Of course, these solutions sound ridiculously glib to those who are about to jump into the big unknown without a life preserver. And, in fact, when worst-case scenarios come to pass, few of us are able to give the ol' shoulder a shrug and say, "Oh well, forward and onward." No, we tear out our hair, we rave, we rant, we feel ill. It takes a while to move from panic to survival mode, but eventually we do stumble into being able to cope. And if you have the temerity to follow through on a goal, then it stands to reason that you can harness that same steadfastness and faith to rebuild your situation.

The inner champion holds trump cards too

The inner critic may be able to taunt you with a litany of screw-ups in the past, but the inner champion has its fair share of trump cards to throw on the table. As much as we've messed up at times, we've done things right more often than not.

118

Sure, every one of us wishes we were that much brighter and wiser, but we all know from looking around us that you don't have to be an Einstein to be successful. Those with the follow-through factor say that what you do need, however, is the ability to shake off the feeling that you're destined to fail because you haven't met the expectations or standards of others in the past. A standard is just another word for judgment. And people's judgments are usually harsh, and they say more about their problems than yours.

A human resources professional named Karina became a certified business coach so she could expand her role at work and offer coaching. But her skeptical vice-president determined that her training wasn't good enough. "My boss kept holding up these hoops for me to jump through. And every time I'd make it through one hoop, he held the next one higher. After I became certified as a coach, he told me I was unsuitable for the role because I wasn't an industrial psychologist. I started to believe he was right, maybe I wasn't up to standard."

Karina went from dejected to angry after a colleague joked that even if she got her Ph.D. in psychology from the local university, her boss would still reject her, saying, "But Karina, you're not a *Harvard* psychologist." Karina said that's when she stopped letting his opinion affect her sense of self. "I finally recognized I wasn't the problem. This guy just didn't want his employees to get coaching. He was nervous, maybe he was worried they'd all decide to quit because of him. About two years ago, I stopped asking for

119

permission and told him that I'd be offering coaching on a trial basis. Now I'm the company's official in-house coach."

Don't get discouraged, get mad

When all is going well, you can get away with using positive rational thought to stick it to fear and doubt. But, mostly, these two gremlins attack when you've hit a glitch in the road and your defences are down. The minute you're feeling vulnerable, they're stabbing their finger in your chest and jabbering so loudly in your ear that they drown out all logical comebacks. Worn down by their slaps and pokes, you begin to think that your solutions to worst-case scenarios are silly and your list of triumphs is nothing compared to your track record of failures.

At this point, those with the follow-through factor say the only way to fight back is to puff out your chest and get mad. Seriously. When insecurity overwhelms you and you find yourself listing all the reasons why you shouldn't, you can't, you won't achieve your goal, simply stop and scream. To save your idea and your ambition, shout down your doubt. Give it a tongue-lashing, the verbal equivalent of a black-belt karate kick and punch. That's what high achievers do when their inner gremlins threaten their confidence. When you get irritated and angry with fear, it turns from a snarling dog to one with its tail between its legs.

I urge my clients to come up with aggressive battle-cries to fight attacks of doubt and fear. For my part, I growl, "Not this time" whenever my anxieties prompt me to consider abandoning a project midway. For my client Brooke, who went from being a journalist to opening her own media training agency, "Just watch me" proved to be an effective antidote to her insecurities. After my client Marcus was promoted, he would lie awake all night worrying about whether he was competent to take over a marketing department. He only got some rest when he fought back with "I don't (bleeping) care, I'm (bleeping) going for it anyway."

A battle-cry, which is your verbal punch at fear, is different from a positive affirmation. A positive affirmation, in which you talk about an accomplishment as if you've already achieved it, activates optimism. In turn, optimism creates a powerful energy that fuels action. Affirmations do work, but they're a hard sell to the self. I can repeat that I'm prosperous twenty times every day, but if every time I say it an inner voice mumbles, "Great, so show me the money already," I'm going to have a tough time flicking on the optimism switch.

A verbal punch doesn't ask you to convince yourself of anything. Instead, you're just telling your inner critic to stuff a sock in it so you can proceed with your plans. It's no different than a competitive downhill skier screaming "Shut up" at a scaremonger who is yelling from the sidelines, "Be careful, you've fallen before," and "Oooh, watch for those little bumpy things." Imagine what you'd think if the racer turned to the nervous little observer and said, "You're right,

I should proceed with utmost caution. As a matter of fact, I think I'll do the really safe thing and take off my skis and ride the chairlift to the bottom. Thanks."

Everyone worries that the skier they're cheering could wipe out during the race, but worse than witnessing the fall would be to witness a surrender to fear and doubt. If the skier falls, we still admire her for trying. If she doesn't try, we don't see much to admire. Anyone who wants to make their idea happen is no different than the skier who must tune out fear and criticism to have any hope of success. Like the skier, there are times when you have got to tell your inner scaremonger, in no uncertain terms, to go play in traffic.

CUE CARD

- Fear is like your own personal crossing guard. It's so bent on protecting you that it would keep you standing on the sidewalk forever if it could.

- Self-doubt is fear's best friend. The inner critic reminds you of past failings so you don't get cocky about taking risks. Those who follow through aren't without fear and doubt, but they have learned to shut them out.

- When you're thinking of relinquishing your ambition because of fear and doubt, don't argue or debate with yourself. Get mad instead.

- Push back against your inner scaremongers with a verbal equivalent of a karate punch whenever you need to. When you get irritated and angry with fear, it turns from a snarling dog to one with its tail between its legs.

Two anti-bullying strategies to use on your inner critic

Consider your inner critic – that grating voice of doubt that loves to remind you of your flaws and inadequacies – as your personal schoolyard bully. It's always there, scowling and taunting, in the dark reaches of your mind. The following two exercises will help you move ahead with your ambition, despite the efforts of your pet bully to keep you cowering in your safe corner.

Strategy # 1 – Fight back

Arguing with your inner bully is a bit tricky. You can easily slide into an endless round of finger-poking back and forth. "Am not an idiot." "Are so." "Not." "So." Frustrated and exhausted, you drown out the argument by turning up the volume full blast on *America's Funniest Home Videos*. And that's when the bully gets in the devastating final "Told you so."

The inner critic never gives you the last word. It's like the scorpion in the famous fable that begs a frog to carry it across the river, promising it won't sting it. But it does sting the frog along the way, and they both drown. "Why did you do it?" wails the frog with its last breath. "Because it's my nature," replies the floundering scorpion. It's the nature of the inner critic to criticize. But you can get it to shut up with a verbal punch that leaves it speechless, and a little stunned. This tactic will allow you to slam the door on doubt, or shout it down, whenever you need to.

The absolute best fighting-back technique is to be ready with your verbal punch the second you hear that inner voice declaring that you are incapable of carrying out your ambition. You may already have a favourite "Don't mess with me" line to use. But if you don't have a closed-fisted, eyes-narrowed, teeth-gritting threat to deliver, try this two-step exercise.

1. Think about how your inner bully taunts you. What is a typical self-criticism that triggers feelings of doubt or fear?
2. Instead of giving in to the inner bully, get mad. Think about a scene in a movie, book, or song where the tough guy or gal, all guts and no fear, gets off that perfect "Make my day" line. The hero is intense, serious, angry, and won't back down for anything. That's the moment you want to make your own. In a showdown between you and your doubt, who are you going to let win? Write down what you would say to a taunting bully who wants to take you down.

Strategy # 2 – Unmask the bully

Another technique for tackling the inner critic is to demystify it. Like all bullies, the inner critic is a Wizard of Oz of sorts – a puny, sheepish little guy hiding behind a forbidding mask. It can be very useful to shine a light on your bully to see what this gremlin who has such influence over you really looks like. If you can give your inner voice some physical features, you can more easily see it for the killjoy that it is.

125

1. Pick up a pen and fill in the face that is outlined on the next page. As best you can, draw the features of a person who is always convinced they're right and you're wrong, who is always critical and sees only your flaws and shortcomings.

   - What would the eyes look like?
   - What expression would he or she have?
   - What hair would he or she have?

Write down what the inner critic is saying in the bubble. In the box, write a retort to shout down this bully.

2. Looking at your drawing, ask yourself these three questions:
   - Does this critic really want to believe I can succeed?

     Yes / No

   - Does the critic want to encourage me to try?

     Yes / No

   - Does the critic want to support my decision to go after my goal?

     Yes / No

3. Every time you hear the voice of doubt, think of the disapproving face of your inner critic and tell yourself, "I'm not going to listen to that part of me that doesn't want me to even *try* to succeed.

Fight Back _____

_____

_____

_____

_____

_____

Yes, but I don't have the time

Ideas have a best-by date. You think you can safely put one in a drawer until later, but by the time "later" comes, if it ever does, you'll open the drawer to find there's nothing in there. The idea you thought would be waiting for you evaporated into thin air long ago.

An idea is like a smouldering ember. Blow on it, and it'll get red hot. Leave it alone, and the fire goes out. "Wait," you challenge. "What about people who have lifelong dreams to sail around the world or compose an opera, and finally get around to doing it at ninety-one years old?" First of all, those people never stopped blowing on their ember. They researched, they planned, and they worked at the skills they needed. Secondly, if they had moved a little more quickly, they could have sailed around the world more than once, or written a dozen operas. So while they are inspiring, they may not be the perfect role models for you.

Rarely do the planets, stars, and your free time line up in harmony. There's always a reason why next year, or the next decade, might be better timing for you. If you have some rock-solid reasons for putting off your ambition, then at least make sure you carve a start date in stone and keep blowing on your ember until then. Maybe it doesn't make sense for you to take Alfie out of high school and tent-school him while you spend a year camping in the rainforest of Madagascar, tracking lemurs. Of course, it might be an amazing year, but let's say it would hurt Alfie's chances of a hockey scholarship for university. Don't put the entire venture on hold until Alf is wearing his NHL jersey. Instead, put in place a step-by-step action plan that keeps you moving towards a departure date that works for everyone.

Time is an odd thing. The years between the ages of ten and twenty-one are a lifetime. To the twenty-one-year-old, his or her tenth birthday wasn't just yesterday. To the ten-year-old, it doesn't seem just a few months between winter one year and winter the next. What whizzes by for the adult feels like a long twelve months to the child. But our feeling that time is picking up speed as we age isn't just a fanciful notion. Our sense of time changes as we get older because each year becomes a smaller piece of the pie, mathematically speaking. To the ten-year-old who has lived 3,650 days, one year is ten percent of his life. To the fifty-year-old who has 18,250 days under her belt, one year is but two percent of her life.

The days and months go by so fast that it feels like we're all travelling on a high-speed moving sidewalk. Don't follow through on your idea, and in a mere two percent of your life, you'll already have moved far away from it.

The clock is ticking. Literally. There's something called a death clock on the Internet that takes into account a few factors to estimate your actual checkout day from Hotel Earth. Then the clock starts counting down the number of seconds you have until your departure. Nothing gets you to panic and move on your list of a hundred things you want to do before you die than seeing the seconds left in your life tick away before your eyes.

But the fact that no one can afford to put life on hold is not the only reason to move ahead on your goal today. The other reason is that ideas go stale if they are not activated. As the heat leaves the ember, energy seeps out of an idea and leaves it cold. Eons ago, my sister and I were both hurting after our respective boyfriends gave us the heave-ho. To console ourselves, we began co-writing a funny book on how to survive a breakup. We were off to a great start, killing ourselves laughing as we wrote page after page on how to recuperate from dweebs. And then we let life get in the way. A couple of large assignments fell from the sky and we bumped *Take Two Brownies* right off our timetable. It was years before we got a lull in our schedules, and when we did, we wanted to put our energies into something fresh and new, not dust off yesterday's news that had been sitting in a drawer forever.

While we were in the process of writing the book, each chapter sparked ideas for the next one. Everything we did and saw stimulated our thinking. We'd see greeting cards in drugstores and rewrite the romantic ones on the spot, changing "I love you more than anything" to "I love you more than . . . well, a really bad migraine, maybe." We'd sing over the songs on the radio so "I can't forget you" became "I can't forget the $220 you owe me." Riffing ideas kept our fire for the project burning.

When we stopped working on the book altogether, we stopped all that spontaneous brainstorming. Our focus changed. We got too busy. And much later, when we toyed with reviving the project, we found we'd lost the momentum. If we had kept blowing on our ember of an idea, even for just an hour a day or a day a week, we'd now be the creators of a book that might have inspired a few broken hearts to repair faster.

The reason it's so tough to pick up your project where you left off is because you've changed and grown over that time but the idea that you wrapped in plastic and put on the shelf hasn't evolved with you. My sister and I got over our heartbreaks. We had moved on, and we didn't want to return to the past. In fact, over time, we rewrote history so that years later we were convinced that we were the ones who had dumped the twits. If we had continued working on the book at the time, we'd have documented the bittersweet healing process. The book would have grown with us. As it was, when we dusted off the pages many years later, we didn't feel connected to them anymore.

131

Your everyday experiences and thoughts give shape to an idea

Without your ongoing attention, an idea loses its form, like a plant that wilts when you stop watering it. But for now, you really are too busy to think about your project, right? Hey, what can you do – a day has only twenty-four hours. You've got so much on your plate, you barely have time to shovel in an egg-salad sandwich in the course of the day, let alone futz with shaping an idea you have. This may be your reality, but it's also yours to change.

One thing we know for sure is that when something is important enough to us, we make the time for it. When our jobs require us to take a course of some kind after work and pass a series of exams, somehow we do it. When you believe that your kid is the next Yo-Yo Ma, you somehow find the time to chauffeur him to endless cello lessons and music competitions.

Every minute of the day, you're choosing how to use your time. So here's the question that will determine the life or death of your idea: Do you want to choose to make some time for your project? Answer only with a "yes" or "no." "Not right now" means "no." "I will, next year" means "no."

People who follow through accept that it's now or never. Because it is. You either tend to your project or you let it go. The odds are that you won't ever go back to it, because there will always be new preoccupations that come between you and your idea. Like everything else, ideas age, and an old idea is like an old crush. When you meet up with it again after years, you can't quite remember why you were head-over-heels infatuated. You're no longer sure what set off the little sparks, and what vision of the future you had in mind back then. When you stay with the idea, the details and the vision stay with you.

A common reason why people don't stay with an idea is because they fear it will take too long for them to bring their goal to fruition. I overheard the best comeback to this concern in a little crammed bistro in Brussels, where I was enjoying the city's famous French fries while eavesdropping on a conversation between a woman and her elderly mother. The daughter was trying to decide whether to go back to school to become a pharmacist.

"It's a good profession," said the mother. "You'd like it. And you're so unhappy as a nurse."

"But *Maman*," said the daughter, "it's a crazy idea. Do you realize it'll take me four years of study? I'll be forty-two when I graduate."

"But *ma chérie*," said the mother, "in four years, you'll be forty-two whether or not you become a pharmacist. Why not be forty-two and a pharmacist instead of forty-two and still miserable?"

"She's right," I blurted. The mother looked over and beamed at me. She and I became fast friends, and her daughter decided to go back to school.

Time is going to pass regardless of what we do with it. We might as well use the time to get someplace we'd rather be.

133

NOTE TO SELF: Fatalists will tell you that if you don't revive an idea you've put on ice, it wasn't meant to be. That's just a story people sell to make you feel better about not following through on your ambition. There's no reason to think that the energizing idea that you didn't explore wasn't worthwhile. Your idea didn't materialize because you got distracted, moved on, and, in time, found yourself in a different frame of mind. You can say you made a choice not to pursue the venture, but you can't know for sure that it wouldn't have been an interesting road for you to travel.

Consider what you're saying "yes" or "no" to

There are hundreds of books and courses on time management. I've read most of them, and taken more than a dozen workshops on the subject. I've never found a one-solution-fits-all answer. For some of my clients, dividing the day into blocks of ten or fifteen minutes works. Iris, a computer programmer whom I coached, was able to write her novel at her cubicle during her lunch hour, five days a week. She transitioned from her job to her novel and back to her job without missing a beat. I was envious of her ability to ping-pong back and forth. Another client, who wanted to run a marathon, took me up on my suggestion of starting her mornings at 4:15 and training until 7:00 a.m., when she had to get her kids up and get herself to her job. She did that for two years and completed the Boston Marathon. I couldn't have lasted a week on that schedule.

I've tried every time management strategy that I recommend to clients. Delegating tasks to others, going to bed later, getting up earlier, making to-do lists for the day, week, and month, or setting a timer are all terrific if they work for you, but they don't happen to work for me. The only method I've found to be effective is to ask these two questions: What am I saying "yes" to? What am I saying "no" to?

These questions get you off the hamster wheel and thinking about what is meaningful use of your limited time. What's going to make you feel better about yourself and your day? Saying "yes" to lunch with a colleague who is probably just going to gripe about his latest home renovation crisis means saying "no" to an hour of work on your project. Saying "yes" to finishing an article means saying "no" to checking and responding to email every five minutes. Saying "no" to looking online for cheap hotels in Rome, in case you ever decide to go there, means saying "yes" to completing your tax return.

If you have faith that your project is a worthwhile pursuit for you, then use the micro-step plan (at the end of this chapter) to figure out which tasks are required to make it happen. Put the idealist in you aside and schedule these activities into your day or week in a way that's realistic. If you really aren't a morning person, chances are you'll just keep hitting the snooze button when the alarm goes off at five in the morning. By seven you'll roll out of bed with a massive headache from being startled awake every ten minutes for

135

the past two hours, plus you'll be mad at yourself for yet again failing to get up in time to work on your project. Say "yes" to sleep and "no" to beating yourself up. Instead, work on the project for half an hour at ten o'clock every morning, or dedicate three lunch hours a week to it, or set in stone specific hours on the weekend.

It's critical for the time-challenged to assign specific times on designated days to their project instead of waiting for a hole in their schedule to miraculously appear. Holes in schedules don't actually exist. Just when you think you have an open slot, a demand comes along to fill it. And demands are like whack-a-mole games. You no sooner bop one back into its hole than ten others pop up. But if you schedule your project into your life as you would a series of dentist appointments, you'll make more progress than you can possibly imagine.

Don't fly standby

More often than not, our inclination is to put our plans and ambition on the back burner while tending to other people's needs. It's as if we're issuing ourselves standby tickets while making sure everybody else boards the plane ahead of us and gets where they want to go.

Typically, we are far more considerate of others than we are of ourselves. Most of us would like to think the only reason we put the interests of everyone else before our own is because we are just so darn altruistic. And as we juggle the needs and demands of family, friends, and work, who can tell us we're not? But one or two tequila shots into a conversation about our sacrifices, and we start to talk a different story. It's far easier, and a lot less risky, to plan the lives of other people than to plot our own.

It is certainly gratifying to help the people in our world achieve their goals. If it means we remain in the stands and watch while others move forward, so be it. At least we can enjoy anticipating how the people whom we have supported will thank us when they step up to receive their awards. There's just one little problem with this scenario. We're letting time run out on equally important people who could also use a hand – ourselves. And, over the years, we transition from feeling magnanimous to a mite resentful.

Contrary to popular belief, honouring your own interests doesn't have to cost others theirs. In fact, giving your personal goals priority status can prove beneficial to people around you in surprising ways. As they adjust to your agenda, they unfailingly discover that they are more resourceful and better able to problem-solve to meet their own needs than they imagined. In the same way that people who stub a toe curse less if no one is around to hear, people who don't have you at their beck and call, call less and get by just fine.

NOTE TO SELF: Avoid telling people that you didn't fulfill your ambition because of their demands on your time. No one will take the rap for your frustration. Instead of an apology or any kind of sympathy, you'll get a lecture on how you should have planned out your life better. Those you blame will tell you of friends who had equally hectic schedules but still managed to achieve their goals. They'll remind you that bestselling author P.D. James started writing her crime novels while working full-time and caring for her children and ill husband. They'll hit you with, "No one asked you to be a martyr." And to add huge chunks of kosher salt to the injury, you'll have to admit, if only to yourself, that they're right.

Those with the follow-through factor insist that there is no other option but to say "no, not now" to some everyday routines or requests so that you can say "yes" to your appointments with your projects. Everyday needs and demands, like ocean tides, never stop, so it's up to you to step out of the water on occasion.

The minutes and hours of each day are what make up your life. Your life and your time are one and the same. So guard your time and spend it thoughtfully. If you have an idea that you want to pursue, give it the time it needs right now, because a good life is made up of moments that are meaningful to you.

CUE CARD

- The time is never ideal, but you don't have the luxury of putting your idea on hold, because ideas expire if left unattended for too long.

- If you can't activate a major aspect of your project now, carve a date in stone for when you can. In the meantime, keep developing components of your plan.

- Schedule in time on your project as you would a series of dentist appointments that you can't miss.

- If you don't think you have a moment to spare, remember that what you do with each moment is always a matter of choice. Take stock of what you're saying "yes" to, and what you're saying "no" to, throughout the course of your day.

The micro-step plan: Less is more

Why micro-steps?

This template for a micro-step plan (MSP) is one of the best things you can use to help you reach your goal. The MSP works because it's not based on what you *should* be able to accomplish in a given period of time, but instead on what is realistic to expect of yourself given the many demands on your time.

The smaller your expectations, the more you'll get done. If your task is bite-sized and well defined, the odds are good that you will accomplish it and move on to the next one. The bigger and less defined the task, the less likely you'll find the time, energy, and enthusiasm for it.

Moreover, working with a plan that isn't broken down into micro-activities is like unpacking a do-it-yourself treehouse kit and finding it doesn't come with an instruction manual. You have a big picture in mind, but you're not really sure what goes where and how. As a result, the project that you thought would be so doable is now overwhelming.

Think small – very small

The most common mistake people make in writing out plans is thinking too big. They break their action plan down into a few lofty tasks without indicating the micro-steps required to get from one milestone to the next. Their plan may leap from the task of developing Web copy to the task of contacting forty potential clients, with nothing in between. This isn't a plan, it's an oversimplified, self-defeating road map that, more often than not, will get you nowhere.

The challenge of a good plan is to break every major task into its many small components. Identify a particular milestone and then work backwards, asking yourself what all the activities are that you need to do to reach that milestone.

For example, my milestone is to contact forty potential clients. Thinking in micro-activities, I ask myself, "What do I need to do to successfully reach those possible clients?"

Micro-step 1: I must conduct online research to compile a list of forty contacts, with email addresses and phone numbers.

Micro-step 2: I must draft an introductory message for those people I plan to email. For those I intend to call, I have to script a message to leave on voice mail if they don't pick up their phone.

Micro-step 3: I have to set aside a time to send out the emails and make the calls.

Micro-step 4: I need to draft a second message to send to those who didn't respond to my first contact.

Be realistic – very realistic

A plan that sets you up for success takes into account that every micro-step along the way, no matter how small, demands time and attention. With that in mind, the MSP goes beyond regular planning tools by asking you to realistically predict how long each task will take and to specify the day and time when you'll likely be able to complete the activity. In this way, you book engagements with your project as you would book a series of appointments with your chiropractor.

If you were to tell yourself that you'll get to your doctor "sometime" during the week or month, you'll likely never get there at all, despite your good intentions. In a busy life, "sometime" is a euphemism for no time. Whereas when you make a date, you make an agreement. You either honour the date or, if necessary, reschedule it. The third option is to look at your daybook, notice your appointment, and choose to ignore it. But that's very different from just forgetting about it in the course of a hectic week. To ignore it is to make a conscious decision to disregard an agreement you made with yourself. It forces you to consider what you're choosing to do instead that's more important. To forget is to fail to even think about the choice you're making; it's an act of mindlessness.

A plan is no place for optimism. To schedule effectively, you must be extremely pragmatic. The Yes/No column in the MSP acknowledges that you have many demands on your time and asks that you predetermine which interruptions you'll say "no" to and which you'll allow. By making thoughtful decisions on how you want to use your time, you stay in control of your schedule.

For the milestone "Develop Web content," your MSP might look something like this:

Milestone: Develop Web content

Micro-steps	Required time	Date and time	Yes / No	Done
What do you need to do to reach your milestone, and why you need to do this step?	Overestimate time required to complete the activity.	When can I fit this in? Stay realistic and determine not just a day but also a time during that day to devote to this activity.	During the designated time, what am I prepared to say "no" to? Which interruptions will I allow?	Check off what you did to show follow-through
1. **Review websites** of ten competitors to determine the sort of info they include, their unique selling points, etc.	3.5 hours	Mon., Feb. 8 Noon – 1 p.m. Wed., Feb. 10 8 – 9 a.m. Fri., Feb. 12 2 – 3:30 p.m.	Have lunch at desk. Yes to calling home. No to email Have coffee at desk. No to email. Yes to calls from accounting.	✓ ✓
2. **Figure out section headings and key messages** per section. What do I want people to take away from each page?	1.5 hours	Mon., Feb. 15 8 – 8:30 a.m. Wed., Feb. 17 8 – 9 a.m.	Arrive at office early. No to email. Coffee at desk. Take 5 min. at 8:30 to check email.	✓ ✓
3. **Write "About Us"** (about 200 words)	1.5 hours	Thurs., Feb. 18 8 – 9:30 a.m.	Read emails at 9. No calls.	✗ Reschedule Fri. 19, noon – 1:30

One MSP at a time

A threat to any project is our tendency to stand at the bottom of our Everest and wonder how we're ever going to make it to the top. It all seems too unlikely. The solution is to take our cues from long-distance runners and cyclists, who think only about making it to the next milestone, not about reaching the finish line.

If, on the first day of a university degree program, we were handed all the books to be read for all our courses over the next four years, as well as a list of all the essays and assignments to be completed and all the material to be memorized for tests, we'd have a panic attack and drop out before the first coffee break. For that matter, if someone piled three years' worth of your household's laundry at your feet and pointed to a washing machine, you'd feel the same sense of doom.

A project is no more overwhelming than many of the other things we tackle in our lives. The trick is to approach it the same way we approach most of our regular activities: we figure out what needs to be done in the here and now, and we do it. Write just one micro-step plan per milestone at a time. When that milestone is reached, write the MSP to get you to the next one. This is the only way to climb a mountain.

ELEVEN

Yes, but I don't have the energy

Martha is a self-described sloth who has nonetheless managed to fulfill her ambition. Anyone who wants to follow through on anything should put up a poster of Martha, reclined, as always, on her couch and looking weary. For encouragement, you can't do better.

If Martha, who easily and often runs out of energy, can make the transition from holding a full-time job in marketing to running her own business as a Web consultant, then anyone with a pulse should be inspired to kick-start their ambition.

When I first met Martha, I thought the same thing you may be thinking. Easy for her to amble towards her ambition; she doesn't have to deal with a chaotic household, a mother who'll throw herself into traffic if you don't call her twice a day, and a boss whose only goal in life is to unload his work on you. But Martha is a patron saint for low-energy folk precisely because she did have to shoulder similar stresses.

145

Martha's success might seem to be a bit of a miracle to those who are too exhausted to pursue their goal. But it wasn't luck or magic that led Martha to accomplish her plan despite being energy-depleted. This heavy-lidded woman, who never met a sofa she could resist, made change happen by harnessing a source of fuel that exists for all who aren't following through on their interests. Martha dipped into the well of frustration. Her profound irritation with her work life invigorated her just enough to put some wheels in motion, albeit in slow motion.

Martha didn't enjoy corporate life, and when she looked to the future, she saw only more of the same. This inspired her to take e-learning courses on web design at night. She was never much of a housekeeper and her place was even more of a disaster during her transition years, when she was learning new skills and experimenting with ways to promote her business. But everyone, including the fish, survived.

Five years later, the state of Martha's house hasn't improved noticeably, and she still would rather nap than work. But now she sets her own hours, and she revels in the fact that she has the option of working in PJs.

Spending time with Martha is empowering for those who are not high-energy types. Tell her the only thing you did at the gym that morning was to buy a muffin at the juice bar, and she'll tell you that anyone who can drive to the gym, find a parking spot, decisively choose a muffin, and get on their way can clearly take on the world. She's a welcome respite from high-octane people whose stories of expanding their business while earning ballroom dancing trophies and fundraising awards, in between hosting gourmet dinner parties, make you want to crawl back to bed and stay there for the next twenty years.

As Martha proves, you don't need to be high-energy to follow through. I interviewed dozens of low-energy types who still managed to complete projects. Did they inject caffeine, take amphetamines, or suck in pure oxygen? No, at least not that they admitted. Instead, they found inspiration in the old story about the tortoise and the hare. Like the tortoise, they paced themselves, moving slowly from couch to computer to bed.

In the fable, the turbo-charged hare races ahead and feels so smug about making time that it stops along the way for a snooze and doesn't wake up until the tortoise has made it past the finish line. Low-energy folk naturally love the part where they leave the hyped-up Type-A whirling dervish knee-deep in their dust or, since they don't actually pick up enough speed to create dust, in their candy wrappers and Styrofoam coffee cups. But of course, in real life, high-energy people don't nap. Luckily, following through is not a race.

In a web-class discussion, Oprah Winfrey recalled that when she first started her own show, she was often asked how she felt she was progressing compared to other popular talk shows of the day. She would dismiss the question by insisting,

147

"We're running our own race here." Oprah clarified that constantly comparing yourself to others drains your energy.

In her book *The Emotional Energy Factor,* psychotherapist Mira Kirshenbaum writes that physical energy accounts for at best thirty percent of your zest, and emotional energy for seventy percent. She argues that if you're running on empty, it's not because you were born with a small fuel tank, it's because your life, for various reasons – such as divorce or a crazy agenda or guilt – has caused a leak in your tank. Ideally, you want to fix the leak, but in the meantime, what do you do when you've got a project to move on? Those with the follow-through factor think small – very, very small.

The Chinese philosopher Confucius said it first when he said the journey of one thousand miles begins with a single step, and added, "It does not matter how slowly you go so long as you do not stop." Over the past two thousand–plus years, everyone from ancient philosophers to today's motivational speakers has weighed in with the very same idea. Through the ages, they've been crying out from the mountaintops, "If you don't have a lot of energy, just take one little micro-step a day." At least, that's the gist of what they've been bellowing.

Now, you may suspect you know better than those sages and remain convinced that putting in just a teensy-weensy effort isn't going to get you anywhere. You figure since you're too busy and worn out to do much, there's no point doing anything. But you can't fight the hard-core science that proves you're dead wrong.

Newton's law can't be denied

Consider Newton's law of motion that states, in a nutshell, "Every action creates a reaction." In other words, if you do something – even if it's not much of anything – something else will happen. But if you don't do anything at all, Newton's law of inertia applies, which states that without interaction of any kind, things continue on exactly as they were: either things stay still or continue to move at the same speed and in the same direction as before.

Clearly, doing more is preferable. It's more satisfying to check ten things off your to-do list in a day or even a week than to make just one little tick on your page over the same time frame. But for the harried and the beat, doing an extra ten tasks in a short period of time is just not feasible. For those folks, one little tick at a time is more than good enough.

Mike, who now runs a German food import business, is proof. A single dad, he was a radio salesperson who was so tired at the end of the workday that it took all his reserves of energy to get dinner on the table, oversee homework, take his sons to hockey, and then do laundry. He was keen on his idea for an online German foods import business, which he would be able to work at from home, but by the time he got through his evening routine, he was too bushed to do anything but zone out in front of the television. More nights than not, he'd fall asleep on the couch and not wake until morning.

We worked out a plan that while Mike was watching late-night sports, he would sit with his laptop and search for

149

websites that would give him the information he needed about importing dry goods, suppliers, shipping prices, regulations, labelling, etc. The deal was that he didn't even have to read the sites; he just had to scan to see if they were relevant and bookmark them. To make the task as painless as possible, we agreed that he would shut off the computer when the sportscast was over, even if he hadn't found anything worth bookmarking by then.

A funny thing happened to Mike as he Googled. He started to get little surges of enthusiasm that gave him small, unexpected blasts of energy. He found himself staying at his desk at lunchtime to read through the sites he'd bookmarked. And one night, he didn't just bookmark a site, he actually read it through to the contact page and fired off an email while the sportscasters were trading football scores. The email he got back prompted him to phone City Hall to find out about regulations for warehousing dry goods in his basement. City Hall told him where to download a form, which he filled out a week later while the sportscasters were talking soccer.

About four months later, Mike stayed up after the sportscasters signed off to bid on a labelling machine on eBay that he'd need for the business. Within five months, he was dedicating every free lunch hour to the business, and his nighttime TV sportscast became background noise while he worked. After twenty months, his German import e-business was up and running.

One micro-action leads to another

Inside even the smallest action there's an energy, which physicists call a force, that will spawn another action or reaction. This is not news to people who work out. I used to go to a gym in the early morning with a bunch of kindred spirits who also weren't fond of greeting the dawn and who would have preferred, a million times over, to have been at home, sleeping. Each of us would step reluctantly onto the treadmill, feeling wiped, done in, dog-tired, or as one guy would always say, "dead – stone cold dead." Daily we'd announce there was no way we'd last more than three minutes. And yet, we always found ourselves jogging for twenty minutes. Once we got started, our energy magically increased.

Those without high-octane gas in their tank who have the follow-through factor speak of two nuggets of knowledge that are like strong hands pushing at their back:

1. Energy creates energy. One little tiny action eventually unleashed a force they never knew they had in them. Momentum builds, gaining speed and power along the way.

2. A mere minute of visualization can rev up your engine. The feeling you get when you see yourself accomplishing a goal is like a shot of adrenaline.

Visualization has long been touted as the secret to success. The theory is that when you picture clearly what it is that you want, your subconscious works in tandem with your conscious planning mind to make things happen.

When I first learned to drive, my instructor told me to steer with my eyes, not my hands. "Look where you want to go," he would say, "and your hands will move the wheel to take you there." Visualization follows the same principle. Define what you want, see it in your mind's eye, believe that it's already yours, and your creative mind will inspire you to action to get it. This tried-and-true technique, taught by all peak performance experts, is practised by every athlete before an event. It's also practised by those who follow through.

A client named Gemma, who has a high-pressure job in television, a demanding family, and a desire to do nothing but read, is still in awe that she managed to first declutter and then paint her entire apartment. But she loved a picture she held in her mind's eye of herself relaxing in an apartment that looked and felt a lot like a suite in an elegant boutique hotel. That image energized her enough to take the micro-steps she needed to change her reality. At the time, her living room resembled an overstocked used bookstore and her bedrooms looked like roadside junk shops. She began the transformation by doing nothing more than selecting five books every Saturday morning to donate to the library.

On the fifth Saturday, she got the whole family involved in tossing books into boxes to be carted off. On the sixth Saturday, she packed the back seat of her car with bags of magazines, picture frames, lamps, Thermoses, teapots, coats, and old shoes. After a couple of weeks of driving around without being able to see out the back window, she dropped her load at a charity. Now, Gemma tells me, there's nothing on her coffee table but a single candle.

NOTE TO SELF: Half the time we talk ourselves into exhaustion. Try this experiment. Walk into your cluttered office or sit down to ninety-five unopened work-related emails and tell yourself, "God, I'm so tired, I can hardly stand it." Feel yourself getting sleepy, very sleepy. Or how about this: every time someone asks how you are, answer that you're wiped. By nighttime, you'll barely have energy to brush your teeth. Typically, we don't put up a whole lot of resistance to negative thoughts, so they latch on quickly and effortlessly. Meanwhile, a positive thought has to complete an iron-man marathon before we accept it. Still, keep telling yourself, "I'm feeling really good," and you'll feel, if not perky, at least a lot better than if you were to tell yourself ten times a day that you're bushed.

We're as energetic as we think we are. And how we think is easily influenced by what we hear. If, after we pull an all-nighter, colleagues tell us that we look amazing, we'll rev up. On the other hand, we may be feeling great until a workmate clucks, "You look like you could use a holiday." So much for feisty; now we just feel fatigued. To protect your energy, cut short those who always delight in telling you how tired, pale, exhausted, or stressed you look. Try this strategy: say, "Don't worry, it's not just me. The lighting in here isn't flattering anyone."

153

Following through by setting yourself small tasks that are as non-taxing as possible is the way to go if you're easily pooped by the demands of everyday life. But no matter how effective and how feasible your micro-step plan is, it's not going to work if you don't actually take the steps.

Often, people will promise themselves small rewards for taking a micro-step forward when they'd rather be putting their feet up. If you can force yourself to put in thirty minutes of hard labour in exchange for five minutes of face time with Ben & Jerry's Double Chocolate at the end of it, then stock up on ice cream and get moving.

But for most people, the carrot technique stops working after a while. That's because you get to a point where the reward no longer seems worth the effort. Sure, for the first week or so, you're keen to do what you must to justify kicking back with that tub of ice cream. But by the fourteenth day, you're sick of ice cream and fed up with the whole reward system.

Don't let your low energy and your ambition get into a debate

At some point, you need to ask yourself this: "Do I want to follow through on my idea?" If you conclude that you do, your next question must be, "Do I want to take the steps to follow through on my idea?" If you answer, "Yes, I do," the discussion is over. You've made your decision. Once you've got your answer, there's no need to keep asking yourself the same question over and over again. Those with the follow-through factor insist that as soon as you've made up your mind to do something, you must refrain from continuing to quiz yourself about whether you *feel* like taking action.

A competitive rower was one of many who taught me by example how to follow through in spite of being low-energy. Unless he has the flu, Evan is on the lake by dawn, seven days a week. It doesn't matter what time he gets to bed the night before, whether he has a headache, painful blisters on his palm, or an important business meeting later that morning. "If I were to ask myself each morning whether I feel like getting up and going rowing, I'd only be on that lake twice a week, maybe," he said. "But I asked myself whether I was going to get up every morning *before* I joined the rowing club. That's when I asked the question, that's when I thought about it, and that's when I came up with my answer. I'm not going to keep repeating the same question a million times."

Decades ago, long before Nike unleashed its "Just Do It" slogan, a group of professional ballet dancers used those very words to explain how they got themselves to the rehearsal studio every day when their bodies ached and their toes were blistered. "We just do it," said one. "We don't stop and ask ourselves whether this is a good day for us to rehearse. If dancers asked themselves that every day, there'd never be an opening night."

Once you've made the decision to follow a plan of micro-steps, don't ask yourself whether you've got energy to actually do the task of the day or not. Just take the step, even if you yawn your way through it. It's actually less draining to go ahead and do what you agreed to do than it is to debate the question and deal with the guilt of not taking the step.

CUE CARD

- You don't need a lot of energy to follow through because, as science proves, even the smallest action causes a reaction of some kind, so movement is assured.

- One micro-step at a time will get you to your destination, and since follow-through isn't a race, the time it takes you isn't the issue.

- The trick to moving forward, even when your feet are dragging, is to visualize the outcome you want.

- When you decide that you want to achieve your goal, don't repeatedly ask yourself whether you feel up to the task. You already settled on an answer when you determined that you wanted to follow through.

EXERCISE
The newest thing in personal fuel – throwing rocks

Increasing your energy supposedly isn't all that hard, at least not according to umpteen magazine articles on the subject. Apparently, it all just comes down to this: eat better, sleep more, stress less, and exercise daily. What's so difficult about that? Nothing, If you live at the Golden Door Spa in Arizona. But if you don't, you may find you're just a mite too fatigued to whip up seafood paella after a long day at the office, and you're a tad too exhausted to spring out of bed at dawn for a yoga session. The problem is you have to spend energy to get energy, and many of us don't have a drop of fuel to spare.

Luckily, there's an energy-preserving exercise that can be done while sprawled on the couch. I call this exercise Throwing Rocks. It's based on the simple fact that while enjoyable tasks and encounters infuse you with zest, upsetting ones leave you drained. It would be terrific if we could eliminate all annoying people and activities from our day, but that's not likely to ever happen. Still, what you can do is transform the unpleasant into the indifferent.

When you neutralize disagreeable activities, they no longer deplete your reserves. You eliminate the power of the task or interaction to anger, distress, or depress you. In this way, a dreaded activity becomes no different than putting gas in your car at a self-serve on a cold, rainy day. It's not something you enjoy, but it doesn't wipe you out.

Throwing Rocks helps you to keep the fuel in your tank in six easy micro-steps.

Step 1: Get comfortable. Any place, any time, any way you choose.

Step 2: Make a list of all the stressful tasks and interactions that drag you down during a typical weekday.

Step 3: Picture each one of these awful activities as a heavy rock that you carry with you all day in a backpack. You are so weighed down you can hardly shuffle to the coffee shop.

Step 4: Now imagine reaching into your backpack and lifting out one rock. Just one. Think about this rock and answer these questions:

- What unpleasant task or interaction does this particular rock represent?
- What's the purpose of this task or interaction?
- What is it about this activity/interaction that upsets me so much?
- If I decided not to get distressed, what would change?
- What's one thing I could do to make this task or interaction less distressing for myself?

Step 5: After you determine a way to eliminate your distress around the activity, imagine tossing the rock that represents it into a lake. Get rid of it. You'll still have to do the task, but it won't weigh you down and drain your energy when it's not embedded in negative feelings.

Step 6: Don't feel the need to exert yourself by throwing away too many rocks at one time. Just one rock a day or even one a week is good enough. In time, you'll find you have more energy left in the day to devote to the project you care about.

TWELVE

Yes, but I don't have the money

You would do it if you had the money. If you just had the money, finishing what you started wouldn't be a problem. If only you had the money, you would take your idea from A to Z without fail. Does this sound familiar?

For most of us without a platinum credit card, the money we make at work or have saved up is our security blanket. Give that up, and we can't sleep at night. And that's a problem because some ideas do require a cash investment. So where does that leave those who don't have spare thousands under the mattress? It leaves us talking about the great idea we'd carry out, if only we had the money.

Yet there are thousands of people who managed to achieve their goals without ever having had bulging bank accounts. Though it's tempting to grumble that behind every success story is a sugar poppa or momma with their hands in their pockets, it's just not true. All those rags-to-riches stories are proof that it's not money that makes the difference, it's the follow-through factor.

Without a doubt, having a lot of extra money makes starting a business, going back to school, buying a cottage a lot less scary. Those of us without a green security net have to take a much bigger risk. And we ask ourselves how dare we be so bold. We say sensible people build nest eggs, they don't take the eggs and fry them. On the other hand, it's arguable that drawing a big X across your ambition isn't the most sensible way to construct a more rewarding life.

Those with the follow-through factor will tell you that spending money as necessary to advance your goal isn't giving in to a whim or an indulgence. It's an investment in your future. You are building something. And it costs to build. That's certainly nerve-wracking when you're not rolling in cash. You can, nonetheless, justify the spend if you accept that you're developing something worthwhile that is important to you. But here's the small print on a contract you make with yourself: you can put the money towards your ambition if, and only if, you follow through with the plan you have for yourself. If you don't, you're throwing bucks to the wind.

Obviously, if spending on your idea means you can't make your mortgage payment, shelve the idea – for the time being. Go back to the drawing board and figure out a way to make the extra money you need to support your plan (raiding the kids' college fund is not an option). But if you are able to cover necessary expenses and are still undecided about the spend, ask yourself this question: "What is important to my future?"

Dahlia was so frustrated and bored at work that she would get into the subway every morning and, like a heat-seeking missile, search out the sickliest-looking passenger to stand next to. "I wanted to catch a cold or flu bug," she confessed. "Getting sick would mean a break from the office."

When a fever and cough start to sound appealing to you, you know it's time to rethink your life. In Dahlia's case, she hoped to eventually turn her hobby of making accessories from vintage clothing into her full-time work. But to build a demand for her goods, she needed to do some marketing. She had to develop a website. As well, she wanted to use her vacation time exhibiting at some of the larger winter craft fairs in a few key cities. Her plans required cash.

If you were to list twenty of the gutsiest things a person might do in life, withdrawing money from a savings plan to kick-start a new business would probably figure somewhere between running with the bulls in Pamplona and performing stand-up comedy.

Dahlia describes herself as risk-adverse. She wouldn't dream of travelling to tropical places, because the low odds of catching malaria or being infected by some kind of parasite are too high for her comfort. She couldn't imagine throwing caution to the wind and visiting a new hair stylist unless the stylist came with a whack of impressive recommendations. Trying out a new restaurant is about as adventurous as Dahlia likes to be. So the mere thought of withdrawing a hard-earned $15,000 from her savings to put towards developing her dream was enough to trigger a panic attack.

"What'll happen if you don't make this move, but instead keep on as you have been doing?" I asked her.

Dahlia shrugged. "I'll continue to stay at a job I can't stand and I'll make accessories on the side for friends. And I'll continue to hope that word of mouth will spread so that I'll land enough orders to quit the job I can't stand."

"But you figure you can speed up word of mouth if you do some marketing and exhibit at some high-traffic craft fairs?" I asked.

"I think so. I don't have a large network, and most people I know are on tight budgets, so right now there's not much word of mouth happening at all. I believe exhibiting is the right move. I feel it in my gut." Then Dahlia paused just long enough to let doubt creep in. "But, of course, I could be wrong."

"So here's the real question for you," I said. "Do you have reason to believe that this investment would take you closer to your goal?"

"Yes, I think I have to market my accessories in order to eventually become a full-time designer."

I figured sooner was better than later, since Dahlia had to be running out of sick days at work. But still, the next question had to be asked: "If you spend the money to exhibit at

163

winter fairs and yet don't get the results you want, what will you come away with?"

Dahlia grimaced. "Depression, heartbreak, pain, and suffering."

"Well, I'll grant you a little depression and some heartbreak, but you may be overdoing it with the pain and suffering." I was about to quote my friend who annoyingly answered my every complaint with the line "As long as you have your health, you're fine," when it dawned on me that if things didn't pan out for Dahlia, she'd probably try to pick up pneumonia rather than return to work.

"Let me rephrase the question," I tried. "If things don't go as planned, what would be the learning for you?"

It took Dahlia a while to come up with an answer, but finally she said, "I'd get an understanding of what's not selling, and why."

I was thrilled by what Dahlia didn't say. She didn't say that she'd learn she wasn't any good at design or that her concept was doomed. Instead, she echoed the thinking of people who follow through to success – at the very least, she'd come away with critical insight that could help her refine her approach.

Dahlia realized that if she considered the craft fairs as her test market, she'd approach the venture differently. If sales at the exhibits were slow, she would talk to browsers to solicit their opinions on a range of issues, including pricing. Regardless of outcome, she would learn something that would contribute to her business.

Dahlia showed tremendous courage when she sent cheques to two winter fairs to secure exhibition space. She was a nervous wreck, but she profited immediately from the hidden benefit of investing. When you dig into your pockets, you're saying to yourself, and to anybody else who cares to notice, that you're serious about your ambition. For those of us who can't afford to spend frivolously, investment of our dollars is an action that commits us to pursuing our plan. It's easy to let go of an idea that didn't cost a penny. It's much harder to drop a ball for which you've paid dearly. Dahlia persevered through four tough years before she got to the point where she could quit her job and make enough money to get by on her craft.

An ambition is like a baby: it takes time and money to nurture it

Those with the follow-through factor think of their project as another child in their family. Without taking anything away from the other children, they need to pay for the new kid in their life – and find hours in the day to care for it.

Some of my clients drop from full-time to part-time work to free up their time for their projects. And they do feel the financial pinch. Even those who are able to live off their savings or their spouses for a while say they get sweaty palms every time they make a cash withdrawal at the bank. And most feel obliged to forego hairdressers or green fees. Some even give up café lattes, although that kind of extreme sacrifice is rare.

There's no denying that people who dedicate their nine-to-five to building their idea often pay the price in anxiety. They fret about money, they fret about dropping out of the rat race, and they fret about dinner, since they can no longer afford to order out for Chinese. Their concerns are not unlike those of a parent who decides to stay at home while the child is little, except those parents can at least sleep peacefully at night because they can defend the financial sacrifice to themselves and to the world. But take a page from their book and consider yourself on parental leave of sorts while you nurture an idea and get it on its feet.

NOTE TO SELF: Spending money on things is more acceptable than spending on ideas. People ooh and aah when you fork out big bucks for a sports car or a wall-to-wall high-definition television, but tell them you're investing money in your ambition, and all you get back is a skeptical "Good luck." It's hard to sacrifice a holiday, a new car, or a move to a bigger house for a dream. No one relishes trading a tangible item, or a cruise on the Mediterranean, for a mere possibility of what might be. But ask yourself this: "Which choice could help me attain the future I want?"

It's stomach-knotting to pay for an ad campaign or a booth at a trade show when you don't have a clue whether you'll make an immediate return on your investment. It goes without saying that you don't want to spend a cent without doing market research to make sure your idea is viable and has a good chance of success. But if you have reason to believe, ask yourself what you'd regret if you didn't go ahead. Building something for your future comes with a price tag, and it can be years before you make your money back. But you also pay a cost for not following through.

When fear keeps you from making whatever purchase is necessary to move forward, take a deep breath and remind yourself why your project is meaningful to you and important to your future. When you have enough money to cover your basics but you're still reluctant to invest a dollar in your idea, your hang-up really isn't the money, it's the dread. What if nothing ever comes of your big plan? What if there's no payoff, not in five years, not ever?

What can you bank on?

People with the follow-through factor are quick to tell you that there are no guarantees. All you can bank on is a sensible expectation of how a particular expenditure may help you advance towards your goal. Sometimes your decision to spend some money is an excellent one, and sometimes your expectations aren't fulfilled.

So let's look at the worst-case scenario, up close. You put money into your idea, you followed through, and you didn't make a penny. You worked full-time on developing an

167

ambition and it didn't pan out. What will happen now? Will you have to move into a cardboard box? Will you never make another dollar as long as you live? No, of course not.

If you give up your job, will you ever find another one? Yes. The law of averages states that if you found one before, you'll find one again. You're not starving now, you haven't starved before, so why would you believe your destiny is to starve tomorrow?

Those who follow through recognize that they are survivors. They know they have the power to make things happen in their life. They dare to spend the time and money they need to follow through because they are certain that no matter what happens, they'll find a way of getting back on their feet. They're not blind to their financial realities. They don't wait until they're almost bankrupt before switching gears and seeking income, but they do give themselves permission to invest in their potential.

The minute you put money into an idea to make it happen, you step onto a roller coaster. But like all acts of follow-through, this ride will take you somewhere other than back to the starting gate, no matter what happens. Following through is like taking a very challenging program of some kind. After you sweat it out, you realize how far you've come and, more important, how much you're capable of.

In a way, you're like a philosophy student. Philosophy is considered one of the toughest disciplines of study. But the question most people ask of philosophy students is not

"What is the meaning of life?" but "Why spend tens of thousands of dollars and dedicate years of hard labour for a degree that leads nowhere?" The answer to that mystery lies amid the statistics collected by universities. Data show that while few philosophy grads end up teaching their subject, most rise to the top in whatever job they do, thanks to their mastery of higher-level creative thinking skills. The study of philosophy doesn't come cheap, but it serves them for life. Similarly, what you learn when you follow through will serve you for the rest of your life.

CUE CARD

- Investing in your idea is not irresponsible or an indulgence. You are building a future. Give yourself permission to invest in your potential.
- While you don't want to bankrupt the family, you may have to consider making a few sacrifices to get where you want to go.
- Growing an idea is like raising a kid: it takes time and money.
- Know that even if the worst happens and you don't get any payback, you'll have learned a lot from the experience, and you'll survive.

169

An exercise in investing in yourself

Following through on an ambition often comes with a price tag of some kind. But there are some things in life worth investing in: a great mattress, a reliable car, exquisite chocolate, a plan that energizes you.

Accountants and financial planners may be the first people to consult when trying to determine how to fund your project. But before you call them, fill out the table that follows.

In particular, consider the spinoff benefits of investing in your idea. Are you investing in a product that may have multiple usages? Are you going to learn a new skill or strengthen a talent that, as well as serving your project, would improve your performance at work and/or your resumé? For example, working a display booth at large, competitive winter craft fairs taught Dahlia a lot about how to sell. As a result of her self-funded experience promoting her fashion accessories, both in person and online, she became a better account manager at work. She was promoted twice before she left her job.

It's possible that you may be able to fund a portion of your project, or all of it, by sacrificing a holiday or a non-essential item – in other words, an indulgence of some kind. Remember, you don't have to give anything up forever, just for now. When considering that trade-off, think of what you get out of that indulgence. Is there another, less costly way for you to gain a similar effect? If it's a change of scenery you crave, could you consider visiting a city closer to home than Vienna this year?

Whenever you're unsure whether to choose your ambition over other options, ask yourself, "Which choice could help me attain the future I want?" There is also a cost to not investing in yourself.

The decision matrix

Required services, products, and/or training	Cost per item	Rationale	Spin-off benefits	Trade-off
List in order of need.		Why do you need to invest in each item on your list? What results do you anticipate?	List other possible professional/personal benefits from investing in this item.	Without jeopardizing your house or kids' education, where could you find the money to pay for this item? What non-essential purchases could you put on hold?

THIRTEEN

Yes, but my gut isn't talking to me

There are times in life when you just don't know what to think. Inspiration has abandoned you; your gut has broken off all communications. You're left feeling as if some kind of internal power switch has been turned off, and you have no idea how to turn it back on again. You're disconnected from your project.

You can no longer tell good work from bad, mistake from success. You leave meetings unsure whether you came off as passionately convincing or wild-eyed and desperate. You second-guess absolutely everything you say and do. You not only worry about whether your presentation sounded idiotic, you drive yourself mad wondering if diving into the middle of the conference table to get the last cheese danish was career suicide. You keep asking yourself questions and not getting any answers.

It seems that just when you're really panicked and more than ever could use a little instinct to fall back on, your sixth sense has upped and gone fishing. Why the abandonment, now of all times? The answer is painfully obvious. It's that knot in your stomach that's muffling your gut. If it weren't for the knot, you'd hear your gut warning you to raise your ridiculously low fees so the client sees you as an expert and not just some newbie who hung out her shingle yesterday. If you weren't so anxious, you'd know to refrain from mumbling to the senior VP as you hand over your departmental plan, "I'm not sure how good this is."

It's a vicious circle. The more uptight and desperate you become, the more you weaken your intuitive powers. And when you're panicked, you can sit in a meeting and coo assurances all you want, but the room is still going to pick up your distress signals. Non-verbal cues, conveyed in tone, pitch, posture, and expression, communicate seventy-eight percent more information than words. The elegant message that took you hours to craft and memorize is completely undone by the sweat dripping off your nose or the please-love-me look in your eyes.

In the book *Destructive Emotions*, psychologist Paul Ekman, an expert in non-verbal communication, notes: "Our thoughts are private; our emotions are not. Emotions are public. By that I mean that we signal to others, in the voice, face and in posture, what emotions we feel."

Hypersensitive? Your instinct is on strike

You've got trouble on two fronts when your body language is signalling to the world that your inner compass, which guides your judgment, is on the fritz. First, you transmit anxiety. Second, your ability to accurately interpret non-verbal signals from others is compromised. A new person at the table shakes your hand, nods, and makes a slight frown while picking up his coffee mug. The intuitive mind might have caught his subtle wince when his hand made contact with the hot cup, but since it's not talking to you right now, you figure the guy's scowl can only mean that he can't stand the sight of you. Offended, you decide you don't like him much either. Whenever he talks during the meeting, you look pointedly at your watch. This is not the start of a beautiful relationship.

In an ideal world, your mind would always be calm and clear. You'd meditate twice daily, each time channelling the genius of a Bill Gates. In the real world, you're too freaked out about the boss or the bills to sit around deep-breathing. When I first started my business, I would regularly throw a yoga mat on the floor, light a couple of candles, play a CD of ocean sounds, and then beg any source of greater wisdom to whisper brilliant next steps into my ear. What I'd get instead was my inner banshee screaming orders to get up and vacuum the dusty floor. Eventually I developed the seven-step program that I describe in this chapter to silence the banshee and commune with my intuition. It wasn't easy, but it was worth it.

According to a foremost expert on intuition, Dr. Daniel Cappon, intuition is "the super thinking that is behind every single successful endeavor." Dr. Cappon, who wrote the book *Intuition: Harnessing the Power of the Mind,* explains that deep within our brains, we hold knowledge that the conscious mind isn't even aware of.

That knowledge is like a huge database. Tap into it and you'll access all of your life experiences to date – in other words, lessons learned, usually the hard way. What's more, you'll also get the benefit of a wealth of stored facts and reams of data acquired by sensory input – that is, information that our eyes, ears, and other senses have recorded too quickly for our plodding, analytical brain to notice. That's not all. Dr. Cappon and other experts say this extraordinary database also holds collective memory, or wisdom passed down through the ages – in other words, lessons our ancestors learned, also usually the hard way.

Intuition hits mostly in the form of a hunch

The experts say a hunch, or a feeling, happens when our minds detect a pattern. Working at hyper-speed, the brain looks to match the signals and experiences of a current situation with a situation that occurred in the past. When our mind finds a fit, we get a heightened sense of awareness and probability. This inspires our thinking and leads to more insightful decision-making. Hockey legend Wayne Gretzky, who was known for saying that he would skate to where the puck was going, is a classic example of someone who works intuitively. He could see patterns.

Effective, persuasive businesspeople also see patterns. They can sit in a meeting and pick up the subtle clues from people around the table that indicate what's really going on in their heads. Your intuitive sense is heightened when you focus on what others are needing, feeling, and wanting. The trick to reading a room is to stay very much in the moment, bringing your full attention to people's facial expressions and body movements, and listening to their tone of voice as well as their words, without any preconceptions. The challenge is ridding yourself of those preconceptions, but it's only in observing without bias that you can see and hear clearly. If you're looking and listening to reinforce preset notions, you'll see and hear only what you want, and not what is.

Clarity is what leads to inspired action. Halfway through a presentation, an intuitive businessperson might decide to toss out a well-prepared strategy and sing an entirely different tune to win over the client. Ask that person later what prompted the sudden change in tactics, and he'll typically answer that he "just had a feeling about it." Probe deeper and you'll find he was being extremely observant.

176

We all have the potential to be intuitive and, theoretically, that even includes your friend who is still giving you Grateful Dead T-shirts for your birthday. But it's a skill that takes work and, above all, desire to develop.

The following seven-step workout program for increased clarity and inspiration is like any exercise regime: it demands sweat and commitment. However, there is one ray of sunshine – you can at least eat while you train.

Step 1: Dive in.

Immerse yourself in everything and anything that is even remotely related to your area of interest. Intuition follows information. Taking in a wide breadth of information does more than increase your knowledge about your work; it exposes you to patterns.

When my PR firm was hired to promote the toy industry, my partner and I threw ourselves into the world of kids. As soon as the ink had dried on the contract, we felt it was our professional duty to turn on the cartoon network and pop Smarties. We stocked up on every food with diabetes-inducing levels of sugar that had funny characters pictured on the packages.

Our mornings at the office passed like an eight-year-old's dream, eating Lucky Charms and Coco Puffs and reading comics. We joined kids in playing the games they played, watched their movies with them, listened to their music, went shopping with them, read what they read, and helped out in classrooms. In the boardroom we might have had purple mustaches from the neon drinks we were chugging back, but we could tell our clients in two seconds flat which ideas of theirs would connect with kids, and which wouldn't.

Our immersion into a child's universe gave us a heightened sense of what kids were thinking, needing, and feeling.

The more information you collect on the big picture, the faster your mind can connect the dots. All of my high-achieving clients are self-declared news junkies. It's their daily habit to look through magazines, newspapers, and websites, although they admit they rarely read to the end of a story. They're really just scanning the horizon. But they take in enough to spot trends and get a sense of issues and events that could make an impact in their field.

Step 2: Ask what others are thinking, needing, feeling.

As a species, we're not particularly great listeners. Ever since we were first lectured about the impropriety of crayoning on walls, we have been perfecting the skill of nodding in all the right places without hearing a word. For many of us, it's now become standard practice to listen superficially while we consider what we think about the speaker, and what we think the speaker thinks about us. In other words, we're hearing our own assumptions, and the rest is just background noise.

To sharpen your intuitive skills, turn off the internal dialogue by asking people questions that get you into their head and out of your own. Ask someone what they're thinking about a proposal, and they'll share their thoughts on what works and what doesn't work for them. Ask what they're feeling, and they'll communicate their enthusiasm or their fears. Ask what they're needing, and they'll tell you what expectations and demands they have to meet. As you listen, notice where their energy surges and dips, watch for their assuredness and their hesitations, catch their smiles and their shrugs.

Unbiased keen observation is the secret weapon of people with a knack for accurately reading people in business, in love, and in poker.

Step 3: Spend your down time playing "what if?"

Consider the loud, argumentative rational mind as an arrogant know-it-all, quick to come up with all the answers and always sure that it's right. The mind can be like a peacock parent who refuses to acknowledge a teenager's wild, but possibly valid, explanations before passing judgment. You need to help it lose its closed-minded conceit so that it opens up to a myriad of signals and possibilities.

Intuition sometimes flies in the face of the logical, so we tend to stifle it rather than listen to any out-of-left-field musings. But, of course, being logical and being right are hardly synonymous. It wasn't all that logical for a North American coffee chain to confuse customers by calling its small coffee cup "tall," its medium one "grande," and its large "venti." But it was certainly an inspired move on the part of Starbucks, one that set the chain apart from the rest and eliminated the chintzy word "small" and the guilt-inducing word "large" from its menu. **179**

To break down the barriers between the rational and intuitive, ask yourself seemingly wacky, off-the-wall questions, like crazy "what ifs?" What if we called a small cup a tall cup? What if we offered this service with some kind of gadget? What if we invited people from uninvolved departments to our brainstorming? What if we promised something nutty to customers? What if we wrote a proposal as if we were addressing kids directly? What if we turned our garage into a neighbourhood art studio?

Any questions that eschew normal standards and traditional logic force you to think creatively, and the creative mind is the home of inspired insight. It worked for Einstein, who famously asked the impossible question "What if I could ride a beam of light?" and came up with the theory of relativity as a result.

Step 4: Break your routine.

We are creatures of habit. We travel the same mile every day, go to the same place for coffee, sit in the same chair, stare out the same window. No wonder we can't hear our intuition – we've bored it to sleep. Routine may be comfortable, but "same old same old" thinking risks stifling our creative juices. New stimuli force new responses. That's why you have to play hooky on a regular basis and do something you don't normally do. Go to the art gallery, see a different type of movie, visit a new neighbourhood, try a new restaurant across town. In doing things you don't typically do and observing things you don't normally observe, your mind works overtime to make connections, which kick-starts your intuition.

NOTE TO SELF: When asking "what if?" don't let yourself, or any-one else, call your question stupid. Everything new started as a "silly" question. "What if we opened a bakery just for dogs and sold $35 birthday cakes for Pluto?" could easily be dismissed as one of the most demented queries of all time. But today, unbe-lievable as it may be, bakeries for dogs are thriving in many large cities. Likewise, don't allow "That would never work" as an answer. Dissing an idea off the top is just too easy. There's no challenge or fun in it. More importantly, it doesn't stimulate cre-ative thinking. Answer your far-out questions from the perspective that anything is possible. For a few minutes, step outside of real-ity with all of its limitations and preconceived ideas. When critics scoff, adopt a superior tone and reply, "To quote Robert Kennedy, 'Some men see things as they are and ask why. Others dream things that never were and ask why not.'" Follow up with Walt Disney's "If you can dream it, you can do it" before ending with a smug reminder from Hamlet: "There are more things in heaven and earth, Horatio, than are dreamt of in your philosophy." That should shut up the skeptics.

Step 5: Take time off.

Intuition needs time and space to roam free. In other words, you've got to switch off your mind and not think about any-thing for a change. One way to do this is to sit and stare. Of course, you might want to limit the amount of staring you do in a meeting or on the subway. People tend to get a tad

181

nervous when you fix unblinking frog eyes on them for any length of time. But in the privacy of your home, enjoy a good hypnotic stare that puts you in that in-between-awake-and-sleeping state. A lot of how-to-be-intuitive books urge that you daydream in the shower or, even better, zone out in a bubble bath. This works, plus you reap the added benefit of smelling of vanilla. If, however, you find it impossible to meditate or zone out, you can always try doodling or flexing your imagination by giving it effortless tasks. Join your kid in looking for animals in the clouds, or imagine what your colleagues would look like if their eyes changed places with their mouths. Imagination strolls arm in arm with intuition, so when you tickle one, you nudge the other.

Step 6: Make some snap decisions.

Start with things that really don't matter. Do you want go to a movie or not? No thinking allowed. Whatever you decide is hardly going to change the course of history, so act on your first impulse and see what happens. It's Sunday – what do you feel like doing? Decide in less than 7.5 seconds, insists Dr. Cappon. He explains that answering quickly doesn't give your logical mind enough time to tell you what you "should" do, so your instinct has a chance to be heard. The objective is to practise going with your gut so that you can learn to trust it. The trust factor is critical because nothing kills intuition faster than second-guessing yourself. And nothing kills other people's trust in you than watching you dither.

When you're about to make a left turn onto a side street from a busy two-way road, you just know when you can safely make the turn and when you can't. You don't sit there idling in the middle with a calculator in hand, figuring out the speed of the oncoming traffic and the distance between cars. You make an instinctual decision based on a thousand experiences of left turns that you could not consciously detail.

Step 7: Visualize, visualize, visualize.

Star in a movie of your mind and see yourself doing exactly what you want to be doing, with others reacting as you hope they will in reality. Visualizing bypasses the rational, doubting mind and puts you in touch with your feelings and your creativity. The trick is, when you come out of a visualization, don't ask yourself the self-scoffing question "How in the world would I ever make that happen?" Instead, ask, "What could make that dream happen?" The answer doesn't need to be feasible to start the intuitive mind ticking. A friend visualized five publishers bidding on his first mystery novel.

"What could make that dream happen?" I asked.

"Let's see," he said, grinning. "Maybe if the five publishers were stranded on a desert island with me and they had absolutely nothing else to do but listen to me."

"So where would a group of publishers be coming from or going to?" I asked.

"Maybe a book fair," said my friend. "You know, I have a lot of airline points. I think I'll go to the book fair in L.A. and see if I can pick up any business cards of agents. What have I got to lose?"

You have different and more inspired dialogues with yourself when you start from a place of feeling good rather than from a place of skepticism, anxiety, and doubt. A distressed mind is like a clenched, sweaty fist: it can't pick up anything.

Intuition is not a rock-solid warranty or an infallible fortune-teller. But it does clarify and sharpen your thinking. It gives you greater insight. Above all, when you and your intuition are talking, you feel a sense of calmness about what you're doing.

People with the follow-through factor say they need to have that feeling of confidence that they're doing the best they know how at the time. They trust themselves, and other people pick up on that strength and respect it. As a result, interactions are more positive, so they feel they can try more things and take more risks.

CUE CARD

- When you find yourself second-guessing everything you do and think, it's essential to take steps to stop the panic. People who follow through know that you need to trust in yourself, and that involves listening to your gut, not just your logical mind.
- Intuitive thinking is really about detecting patterns, which leads to inspired action. When the mind matches a current situation with other experiences you have had or know about, you get a heightened sense of awareness and probability. You see more clearly.
- To gain clarity in interactions with others, get out of your head and into theirs by asking questions about what they are thinking, needing, and feeling and by paying attention to their body language as well as their words.
- When you act intuitively, you feel confident enough to take whatever risks you need to move forward.

FOURTEEN

Yes, but I can't find a mentor

Deep down, we all just want to be mentored. The very idea of a wise soul with great contacts, who wants nothing more than to shepherd us to success, is enough to make us fall to our knees in hope and desire.

You can pay for expert information; you can network and make contacts yourself. But there's no substitute for recognition from someone who knows your work well. The person who tells you that you're made of the right stuff gives you a boost that money can't buy. The power of mentors is that they can see through to the heart of your business – you. You're at the core of every idea, every goal, every ambition.

Lovers come and lovers go, but a respected person who sees your potential is someone you carry in your heart forever. Sadly, there's a shortage of good mentors on the market. Once upon a time, the world was full of corner offices from which grey-haired, warm-hearted men and women

with friends in high places would keep an eye out for pro-
tégés. Nowadays, most who have survived the latest restruc-
turing dye their hair and watch their backs. And a good
number of younger people in key positions are looking to
ally rather than mentor. So where does this leave a person
with an idea and a yearning for help and guidance? Looking
for a mentor in all the wrong places.

In a competitive world, ask someone in your field of
dreams for advice and you'll likely hear warnings about how
tough things are nowadays. A classic line from a seasoned pro
is, "If I was starting out today, I probably wouldn't make it."

It's a rare person who will spend time, share valuable info,
and make some calls on your behalf. Those who do mentor
know how gratifying it is to help someone eager to learn. But,
unfortunately, you can't call up the president of a market
research agency and tell her that she'll find any time spent
teaching you how to start your own agency really rewarding.

Naturally, you can buy advice. Business consultants and
professional associations are there to fill in for the absent
mentor. These are hugely helpful, but they don't necessarily
make you feel special the way only a mentor can.

Often when following through on something new, you
feel as if it's you against the world. You have to prove yourself over and over again and battle skepticism and rejection.
All you've got is you, and it can get lonely – like piloting a
plane solo at midnight when you're not sure where the nearest airport is and there's no one on the other end of the radio.

Like that pilot, you're not going to just give up, but your confidence can dip dangerously low. At times like that, if you don't have a mentor, the only thing to do is make one.

The do-it-yourself mentor

The do-it-yourself mentor starts with you writing down things people have said to you over the years that have made you feel good about yourself. Travel as far back in time as you can – perhaps even to the Grade 5 teacher who praised you for your thoughtfulness.

In my case, a line from a crabby, arrogant professor is etched forever into my brain. The man taught creative writing at the master's level and led a not-for-credit summer workshop that I took about twenty-five years ago. He looked as if he'd be a lot happier plucking wings off flies than listening to a group of hobby novelists read out their earnest late-night scribblings. But since he was stuck with us, he ripped our precious paragraphs to shreds instead. So it came as a complete shock to me when on the last day of class he approached me at the coffee machine and muttered, "For God's sake, stop second-guessing yourself all the time. The only thing between you and success is faith and commitment." Those few words changed me. Until then, I was absolutely convinced that I owed any success in the writing department to fluke, not skill. (Of course, I completely blew the moment by responding, "You're not just saying that to be nice, are you? No, of course not, you're not that nice.")

For most people I've surveyed, it's a challenge to come up with a long list of positive remarks that mean something to you. In part, that's because a source has to be credible for us to take a compliment to heart. It's nice of a colleague to rave about an article you wrote, but it's tough to get excited when you consider this same person wasn't kidding when she said the best writing is to be found inside fortune cookies.

Mostly we're all far too quick to dismiss kind remarks made about ourselves, although we brood forever on criticisms, no matter how small. The true value of a compliment is heightened when you consider that, unlike words spoken in anger, praise is not thoughtless. Instead, people pay a compliment when something about you, or about what you did, touches them in a positive way. And according to Dale Carnegie, author of *How to Win Friends and Influence People,* we typically get more compliments than we even realize. Just having someone come up and say, "Hey, I remember you" is a morsel of admiration you can take to the bank. "If you remember my name," wrote Carnegie, "you pay me a subtle compliment; you indicate that I have made an impression on you."

Nonetheless, if you still have trouble coming up with a list of kudos that carries weight with you, don't fret. You can fill in the blanks with any encouraging reactions you've noticed from people whom you consider wise.

Think of a time when you won over a tough crowd. Maybe an impossible client signed on the dotted line. Maybe a

189

highly esteemed but priggish colleague grudgingly agreed with your point of view. Perhaps someone who rarely takes calls took yours and kept you chatting. These are not crumbs; these are vitally important bits of material for your make-your-own-mentor project.

If your make-a-mentor project were a collage, it would be a patchwork of wins and insightful, encouraging comments that people have made about you. If the art could talk, it would sit you down and tell you just what it thinks about you. It would say that over time it has listened and watched you and it can see that you have some impressive qualities. It would add that it has every reason to believe you can carry off whatever you want. If it had a phone, it might call up its pals and sing your praises to them. But since it can't talk, all you can do is hang your work and look at it to remind yourself that there are people out there in the world who have taken stock of you, liked what they saw, and figure you're good to go forward.

But what, you ask, about all the negative comments you've accumulated over the years? Don't these make chopped liver of the homemade mentor? No, because the people who do the insulting are rarely credible sources. Oh sure, they may have good jobs and even a few awards on their shelves, but they don't have X-ray vision. These people typically make snap judgments based on superficial, unimaginative criteria. You didn't close the sale – you're no good. You blush at a meeting – you're a wimp. The client doesn't like the copy you wrote – you're incompetent. They can't see past the issue to the talent that lurks behind.

A weakness is often a strength carried too far

Trace a weakness to its source and you'll find a good intention that may simply need to be better managed. The person who isn't adept at closing sales may be fantastic at understanding the perspective of others and doesn't like to impose his own point of view. The gal who blushes may be as smart as a whip but cares too much. The client who hates the ad copy could be stuck on a particular concept and isn't open to your innovative thinking.

The anti-mentors who sit up on their pedestals and criticize your perceived weaknesses are not the best judges of character. No matter how sure they appear, their opinions are influenced by their own impatience, short-sightedness, or even insecurity. Just as the perfect bodies we drool over in magazines are often the ones with the eating disorders or inflatable parts, the arrogant critic is often a closet self-doubter. They fake a lot. It's the nervous Nellie who attacks when you mess up. A confident, wise person doesn't freak out. She can analyze your mistakes, identify your strengths, and advise you how to build on them. She knows that a flaw is almost always a power source that has shorted.

191

I had a client named Pascale who reluctantly quit daily reporting because the city editor told her she wasn't aggressive enough to be a big-city reporter. Feeling like a complete failure, Pascale took a job on a weekly community newspaper. But writing fluff pieces about local businesses that advertised in the paper made her stomach churn. Next, she landed a gig as editor of a corporate newsletter for which all articles had to be submitted to a nitpicking approval process. That job was her idea of hell. No wonder Pascale wasn't thrilled with her job choices; they all flowed out of one editor's flippant judgment of her. I asked Pascale if it was at all possible that that editor had read her wrong.

"Nope," Pascale insisted. "She had my number all right."

"Is it that you found it hard to ask tough questions?" I wondered.

"I don't relish asking offensive questions, but I did when I had to," replied Pascale.

"Did you leave information out of your story because you worried it would upset someone?" I asked.

"No."

"Did you often come back from an assignment empty-handed, with nothing to write about?"

"Are you kidding? I was too terrified of the city editor to report back with nothing."

"So why do you think she said you weren't cut out for big-city reporting?"

"I don't know. I guess she just figured I wasn't right for the part."

Pascale had never questioned the city editor's motives. She just assumed that someone in her position would know what she was talking about. But, in hindsight, she thought about how the city editor, whom we'll call Allie, was notoriously pushy, raucous, and proud of it. Allie had elbowed her way up through the ranks at a time when hard-core journalism was an all-male domain. Pascale recalled that Allie hung out with people in the newsroom who were like her – boisterous, with booming voices and an in-your-face attitude. In contrast, Pascale was reserved, quiet, and soft-spoken. In the end, she acknowledged the possibility that Allie's opinion of her wasn't based on her reporting abilities at all. It could have been that Allie had a tendency to be dismissive of women who don't make their presence felt. Pascale went back to daily reporting at another newspaper, where the city editor had no problem with her quiet diligence.

You've got a choice. You can craft a mentor out of the positive comments you've received or you can dismiss these and believe the negative. But if you insist on listening only to the criticisms, then it's only right to look for inspiration from others who have done the same thing.

Teachers come in all forms – some less charming than others

The official definition of a mentor is someone who serves as a teacher or trusted counsellor. Teachers come in all forms. Your friend who laments that he wanted to become a psychologist, but his sister convinced him that he was too selfish, is your teacher. The bitter executive assistant who didn't go into real estate because her boss warned her that she's not cut out for sales is also a teacher. And the witty guy in purchasing who didn't become a copywriter because an English professor told him his writing was weak is . . . yes, your counsellor. So, too, is the manicurist who pokes a little too hard at your cuticles every time she mentions that she wanted to be a nurse but her mom said she was too scatter-brained.

What are these people teaching? First, that you don't get a lot of sympathy when you gripe over what you didn't attempt because of put-downs. Second, those who define themselves by the negative things people have said about them don't follow through on their ambitions. And are they happier for it? Definitely not.

Ian hoped to start his own business, but his wife, Sheri, was worried.

"Ian, you have to know that you're an idiot when it comes to math," she told him when they were both in my office. "I bet you don't know what 13 times 29 is," she challenged.

Before Ian could finish writing the numbers in the air, I hit the buttons on my calculator and yelled out, "377."

Ian and Sheri shot me a dirty look. I wouldn't be expecting any gold stars from them.

I cleared my throat. "I think what Sheri is suggesting is that you'd need to learn business accounting."

"Learn, shmearn," said Sheri, the disapproving skeptic. "He has no head for numbers. And you have to have a head for numbers to run your own business."

"I could hire a bookkeeper," Ian replied.

"That would be a good move," I nodded.

Sheri glared at me again. "Not good enough. Everyone's an embezzler nowadays. You have to oversee the accounting yourself or you'll be robbed blind. That's why someone like you, Ian, should always remain an employee."

"I can learn how to read account books," said Ian. "It's not brain surgery."

"Maybe not for a normal person, but for you who can't add . . ." said Sheri.

"When someone like me has his livelihood on the line, he's not going to be anyone's idiot. You can bet that nothing will be more interesting to me than a balance sheet," responded Ian. Looking my way, he added, "And nowadays we have things called calculators."

"But you're so not adept," insisted Sheri.

"Yeah, well, I wasn't so hot at parallel parking until we moved onto a busy street. Now I can whip my car into the smallest space and I hardly ever hit a fender. People get better, you know; it's called learning."

Ian had two options at this point. He could have listened to the anti-mentor Sheri, who insisted that he bow to his weakness. She wanted him to agree to her view of him as a guy who is incompetent to run his own show because he doesn't have a head for numbers. Or he could have listened to his self-made mentor. This was the voice inside him that reminded him he has learned a lot of things over the course of his lifetime, and he will continue to learn whenever he is motivated to do so.

Ian went with the do-it-yourself mentor, and seven years later, he's still in business for himself and doing very well. He admitted to me that he's a maniac about overseeing his accounts because he continues to feel he has to prove to Sheri that he can balance a chequebook. Sometimes the anti-mentor can be helpful in her own way.

NOTE TO SELF: A mentor sees that you have possibility. A detractor figures your weaknesses are like flat feet, a curse you're stuck with from cradle to grave. The truth is people develop strength where they need to, when they want to. You might never become a world-class master in your area of challenge, but you certainly can improve dramatically. Music teachers say even people who are tone-deaf can learn to hear pitch if they have proper training. And there are plenty of accident-prone klutzes who eventually manage to rollerblade to work without incurring any bruises or broken limbs.

Mentors win our everlasting gratitude because they're the ones who think enough of us to encourage us to develop our skills. But if we don't have someone to hold our hand, we are still capable of walking, and eventually running, along our path just fine. If you revisit your life, you'll come across so many achievements that you accomplished without anyone's help.

196

Look into even the smallest nooks and crannies of your life and you'll flash on times when you spoke out even though your heart was in your throat. Whether you were a timid high school student who mustered up the courage to raise his hand or an advocate for a cause, you accessed inner strength. Recall incidents when you picked up a phone despite sweaty palms, walked into a room even though butterflies were cavorting in your stomach, showed up for a job that you didn't know how to do, got on a flight when you were unsure what awaited at the other end. When you stop and think about it, there are countless incidents in your life when you have gone ahead and acted even though you were shaking inside. You know better than anyone else how often in your life you didn't succumb to your fears. So while a mentor can be great for helping you recognize your strengths, in the absence of one, there's always the mirror.

The ultimate toast to self

In the early 1980s, when it was still commonly expected for people to partner up before making a major move in life, such as buying a house or taking a job overseas, I went to a radical wedding. My friend Shelley sent out invites that she was getting married . . . to herself. As soon as her pals received the white linen envelope in their mailbox, they were on the phone to each other, trying to figure out how Shelley would handle playing the part of two people at the ceremony. We saw her flinging a jacket on and off over her wedding dress. We had her posing for pictures with her arm around a cut-out of herself. We imagined her hopping from seat to seat when sitting across from the bank manager while being interviewed for a mortgage.

At the wedding, we vowed not to look at each other in case a sidelong glance would unleash a wave of uncontrollable laughter. From that point of view, the event was a dud. Shelley just stood up in her backyard, declared that she would forever more love, honour, and respect herself, and with great flourish, raised a flute of champagne in the air and said, "To me and my future." By midnight, all of us were marrying ourselves and feeling that anything was possible for us.

Sometimes, you have no option but to be your own champion. You have to toot your own horn, no matter how uncomfortable that feels, because if no one else is doing it for you, and you're not doing it for yourself, you have zero source of encouragement. And in the same way that babies become distressed if they are never smiled at, we become despondent if we never receive a pat on the back, not even from ourselves. That pat has more power than you can possibly imagine, because it conveys the knowledge of our potential. And that knowledge is founded on a lifetime of secret and not-so-secret accomplishments.

CUE CARD

- People who follow through don't dismiss compliments they've received over the years, but instead hold on to them like precious gems. They use them as backup fuel whenever they feel their self-confidence is running low.

- Think back over your life and capture the encouraging remarks you're received, the wins you've had, and all the fears – big or small – you've conquered. Together, these make up a do-it-yourself mentor you can trust.

Build your own mentor

When we were kids, it didn't take much to get us to puff out with pride. Something as innocuous as "You did a great job raking those leaves" would make us stand a little taller. Tell us as adults that we did a great job raking, and we toss out an indifferent thanks and a snide comment that we would've done an even better job if we'd had a little help.

Our hearing worsens with age in more ways than one. We stop hearing the small compliments and listen only for the digs and doubts. I recall reliving a day in the life of a client who insisted that not a single person had said one positive thing to him from morning until night. When we pressed the rewind button, we counted up several instances where people showed an interest in what he'd said and thanked him for one thing or another. He was so focused on perceiving slights that he was failing to pick up on any positive reinforcement. It's no wonder that by day's end he was feeling too unsure about himself to draft a proposal to present at a conference.

When you've got everything but confidence, the best exercise is to build a mentor.

To make one, reflect on the compliments you've received, both recently and over time, and jot down the essence of these. Above all, avoid any temptation to be skeptical about the motives of the person who praised you. The Grade 10 teacher who said you have a natural talent for public speaking doesn't say that to all her students. The boss who said he was impressed by your original thinking wasn't just saying that to be nice. There are an infinite number of things people can say; the fact that people chose those particular compliments is meaningful.

Also, think back on the moments of pride and the successes that you've accumulated over a lifetime. These don't need to be Olympian in size to be of value.

Record as many meaningful compliments and wins as you can, and keep these at the back of your mind. Turn them into whispers in your ear when you could use a little boost, a reminder of your many abilities and certain potential.

Things worth remembering

1. I remember, when I was growing up, I felt really proud when I was told

_____

_____

_____

_____

2. When I think back over the past years, some of the wins I feel really good about are

_____

_____

_____

_____

3. There have been times when I felt unsure or nervous, but I didn't let that stop me from

_____

_____

_____

_____

4. One of the nicest things ever said to me was

_____

_____

_____

_____

5. This past year, I felt good about the time when

_____

_____

_____

_____

6. One thing I really like about myself is

_____

_____

_____

_____

FIFTEEN

Yes, but I get so bored

There are two things you have to know about boredom when you're following through on something. The first is that everyone experiences it. The second is that it's nothing to be afraid of. That's good to remember when you're in the grip of boredom and convinced you're going to either go completely out of your mind or roll over and die. Not that you'd mind if you did. At this point, shooting down Niagara Falls in a barrel seems preferable to enduring one more second of ennui.

"I'm bored to death," confessed Ricky. He was suffering through the difficult process of trying to secure funding for his start-up company. "I'm bored thinking about the market, I'm bored looking for investors, I'm bored writing and rewriting the investor relations report. And you know what my partner told me the other day?" he asked, his voice rising in indignation.

"What?" I wondered.

"He said he's sick of hearing me go on and on about how bored I am. He suggested I get a warning tattooed on my forehead: 'Boring person – exposure may induce coma.'"

"Oh. Listen, I'm just going to zip out for a minute to pick up a triple espresso."

"Very funny," said Ricky.

Though boredom can't actually kill you, it has led many to sacrifice their projects to escape from its suffocating grasp. And that's a shame because when you examine boredom up close, you see that it's only a harmless gatekeeper that dresses up in the Grim Reaper's cloak for fun. Push past it and you actually get to the other side of the gate a lot smarter. But let tedium stop you, and you end up empty-handed.

There are a couple of reasons why we always bump up against boredom when we're following through on something. The main reason is that there's typically a lot of grunt work involved in every project. Writing query letters and loan applications, or making lists of possible clients and cold calling, is so tedious that not even buckets of coffee or chili popcorn can pep up the dreariness of our hours. Playing music can help, but it can also be a dangerous distraction if you're prone to picking up a pencil and engaging in a little on-the-spot karaoke.

204 It would be tough enough to get through these chores if we were being recognized for them in some way or had a guarantee that our efforts would end with a win, but most of the time, we're painting in the dark. We often don't know

YES, BUT I GET SO BORED

whether a particular activity will get us closer to our goal. With uncertainty niggling at the back of our mind, it's hard not to click over to the Internet and get caught up in researching how fleas mate or finding out the dog's lineage. But if you do that, you'll fail the gatekeeper's first test.

Trial and error is a boring inevitability

To the gatekeeper's question "Are you scared of dead ends?" the right answer is, "IIa, scared of dead ends. Me? Not in the least. Bring them on." Okay, maybe you don't need to overdo the fake enthusiasm, but you do have to acknowledge that trial and error is part of the follow-through process. What you're doing is no different than the painstaking work of a lab researcher who spends years testing formulas before discovering the right one. You have to exhaust one avenue before trying another. And *exhaust* is the key word, because it can be really tiring. But there are no shortcuts.

Boredom is another word for ennui. And much has been written about what makes us humans regularly drop onto sofas and let out great, weary sighs of ennui. The word *ennui* comes from the Old French *enui*, which also happens to be the root of the English word *annoy*. That makes perfect sense according to behaviourists, who say boredom is a form of annoyance with anything we find meaningless or repetitive.

We tend to think circumstances outside ourselves are entirely to blame for making us restless and annoyed. We figure, change the circumstances and the boredom will disappear faster than free samples of cheesecake. That thinking, say the behaviourists, explains why we're always looking for new toys and experiences to keep us entertained. But, as many a spoiled rich kid has discovered in rehab, shopping and tripping don't work in the long run.

In any event, this quest for variety spells bad news for fledgling projects. Another reason people who have a goal in mind bump up against ennui is because when you're nurturing a new idea, you tend to live, sleep, eat, and breathe it. After a while, it can get to be too much. It's sort of like being joined at the hip with someone, 24/7. No matter how much you love them, at some point they're going to repeat one time too many the same long-winded, not-so-funny joke about three guys in a bar, and you're going to want to go off screaming in the other direction. Similarly, around the millionth time you ask yourself if Pickled Pink is really such a great name for your catering business or if running a contest on your website is a good move or not, you'll start toying with calling it quits instead. You can easily bore yourself into despair by continually worrying the same point to death. That's why those who have the follow-through factor insist that any decision is better than indecision.

When it comes to projects, boredom would not be such a deal breaker if the antidote were simply distraction. But it's not. Here's how you fail the gatekeeper's second test. You tell him you're going to take a break and you'll be back . . . sometime. He'll tell you he won't hold his breath. That's because if you detour off your path because of boredom, the odds are very high that you will not find your way back again.

Distraction is just too seductive to be trusted

It's nice to be preoccupied with something less demanding and more immediately gratifying than whatever idea you've been working on. The symptoms of boredom disappear, your stomach unknots, your foot stops tapping. In your new-found happier state, you find yourself sitting back and wondering if you haven't been pushing yourself too hard, and you advise yourself to enjoy yourself more, to lighten up. Before you know it, the "I'll diet tomorrow" way of thinking takes hold of you.

The problem with taking a mental holiday from a project is that we tend to keep extending the vacation. And we lose all the momentum that we had going. One minute our dining room table is covered with papers, lists, and plans, and the next we've swept everything into a big cardboard box and put it into the basement, "for now." That box might as well be in Timbuktu. Things that go in storage, stay in storage. Storage is where we put stuff we don't want to deal with but feel guilty about tossing. Go check out the back of your closet right now. You'll find a bunch of never-worn shoes that pinch, tacky picture frames, scratchy wool sweaters, and a plastic bag full of half-finished letters, old notes, and yellowing newspaper articles about something you've always intended to follow through on.

207

NOTE TO SELF: There are many people out there who, being follow-through-challenged themselves, are suspiciously eager to support your decision to take a break from pursuing your goal. Admit that you're bored at the moment, and they'll immediately urge you to do something else. We got the message in childhood that being bored is unacceptable. Any kid who ever tossed out, "Ma, I'm bored," would get ten suggestions for what they could be doing fired back at them. Never has a mother been known to say, "That's nice dear, enjoy it." So when you tell pals that you're bored but sticking with whatever you're doing, they go into saviour mode. "Forget about it," they'll say. "You're coming camping for the weekend." Refuse and they'll show up on your doorstep with a shaker of margaritas and some crazy theory that boredom makes for bores. Do your future a favour. Tell them you've come down with the mumps and shut the door on them.

Nix the holiday. The only break you can afford when you're so bored you could scream is ten minutes. In this time, you can power walk around the block, pick up a coffee, or plough through a sandwich. That's all the fun you get. Then it's time to go back to being bored.

Boredom is a lot like flossing. It feels like you're throwing away precious time when you could be doing something much more interesting, like watching the opening monologue of the *Late Night* show. But ten out of ten dentists can't be wrong. They say you've got to floss for long-term gum health. And those with the follow-through factor aren't

208

wrong when they say you have to live with the boredom and stick to the task at hand for eventual success.

Probably there are no greater experts on the subject of boredom than Buddhists and others who practise meditation. If you think people who sit cross-legged for hours on end, counting their breaths, aren't totally bored, think again. One Buddhist monastery has the meditation master whack monks on the back with a stick to prevent them from boring themselves to sleep. In his book *The Myth of Freedom*, the Buddhist teacher Chogyam Trungpa Rinpoche acknowledges that the practice of focusing on the breath for long periods of time is "extremely monotonous and unadventurous." In other words, boring. But ennui always has its rewards.

In the case of meditation, surrender to the boredom and you eventually arrive at serenity. Chogyam Trungpa writes, "As we realize that nothing is happening, strangely we begin to realize that something dignified is happening. There is no room for frivolity, no room for speed. We just breathe and are there. There is something very satisfying and wholesome about it. It is as though we had eaten a good meal and were satisfied with it, in contrast to eating and trying to satisfy oneself." Western philosophers couldn't agree more. German philosopher Friedrich Nietzsche went on record to warn that people who don't let themselves be bored on occasion never experience their own innermost wisdom. Beneath the restlessness there lies stillness. And it is when you break through to the stillness that you experience moments of great clarity.

209

Boredom often leads to breakthroughs

Many in business say they've come up with their best ideas during long plane rides when they'd already seen the movie and had nothing to do but stare into space. Bernie Brillstein, Hollywood's celebrity talent manager, recalled in his book *It's All Lies, & That's the Truth* that when he started out in the business he had no clients, and at the end of each excruciating slow day at the office, he'd go straight home and get into bed. He didn't escape to movies, hang out with friends, or hit the clubs for mindless diversion. He went home and sunk into boredom. And it turns out that was the best thing he ever did. He said he'd get so bored lying around that eventually he'd start analyzing what he'd done right and wrong in his life, until he arrived at the conclusion that he just had to keep trying. Little by little, he built up a business that eventually had stars knocking on his door.

Whether you're counting breaths or staring into space or at a blank computer screen, boredom is boredom. And we all have a tendency to want to escape it as fast as we can. We'll pick up the phone, the remote control, the car keys to save ourselves from the mental and physical discomfort of tedium. But the worst thing to do is give in to this desire, because you won't be running towards anything; you'll only be running away from accomplishing a goal.

Fidgety feelings come and they go. Hang in there just a bit longer than you feel you can stand, and ride through the wave of jittery discomfort that is washing over you. Do not let yourself play online solitaire or post endless comments on Facebook. If you're falling asleep, make yourself a coffee, put in extra sugar, and go nuts on the cookies. Do whatever you need to do to stay with the task you've set for yourself.

One trick that works is to zone out for a minute and imagine yourself celebrating your accomplishment. That's what I asked Ricky to do. I told him to give me the speech he'll deliver, as the keynote speaker at a gathering of young entrepreneurs, after he secures the funding for his business and makes a success of it.

"Now?" he said. "Off the top of my head?"

"Go for it," I said.

"Should I stand?"

"Sure, whatever works for you."

"Do you have a tie I could borrow?"

It's nice to really get into a visualization, but you don't want to spend your short break zeroing in on small, irrelevant details, like what they'll serve for dessert at your award dinner. Stick to focusing on articulating your actual desire.

"Oddly enough, I don't happen to have a tie, Ricky. Anyway, tieless is good. Imagine you're speaking at a weekend retreat."

Ricky stood and cleared his throat. "People," he boomed, "take a look at my knuckles." He lifted up his hand and made a fist. "They're raw. Raw from knocking on door after door after door. Anyone else here have raw knuckles? Let me see a show of hands."

211

Ricky looked at me expectantly. I quickly shot my hand in the air.

"Good for you," he said. I smiled back and rubbed my knuckles.

"It's because I kept on knocking that I'm standing here today," said Ricky. Then he kept on talking, having discovered in that very instant that he loved giving speeches.

Forty-five minutes later, I had to cut him off. "So what are you going to do next time you're going out of your mind with boredom?" I asked.

"I'm going to say to myself, 'People . . .'" His voice returned to a boom, "'let me see your knuckles.'" Ricky smiled. "I love that line. That's what I'm going to use to force myself to keep on slogging."

Those with the follow-through factor know that if you stay with the boredom, in time it will give way to something else. It always does. That's a guarantee. Allow yourself to be bored, really bored, and eventually the panicky, antsy feeling actually retreats and a sense of satisfaction takes its place. It may be contentment from having kept a promise to yourself, or a feeling of hope, a sense of tranquility, or a flash of genius. So when the gatekeeper asks you why you want to push through boredom, tell him it's because you've got a date with something better on the other side.

CUE CARD

- Every project requires some grunt work. And grunt work, which is boring at the best of times, is especially tedious when you're doing it without being sure of a payoff. What's more, thinking about your project all the time can also get a little dull.

- Be prepared to be bored, and don't run from it, because you won't be running towards anything; you'll only be running away from accomplishing your goal.

- Boredom has its rewards. Stick with boredom and in time you'll stop feeling antsy and you'll start to feel a sense of calmness. More often than not, boredom gives way to inspiration.

How to survive boredom

When boredom hits and you want to get away from your project as fast as you can, stay put. Boredom feels like driving through a long, straight tunnel – you see nothing but darkness, you can't pick up a radio signal, and you start to wonder if this particular stretch of road is ever going to come to an end. You can count on hours, days, or even weeks on your journey that will be mind-numbingly dull, but don't make a U-turn. Stay in the tunnel until you see the proverbial light. Meanwhile, try this powerful exercise for sticking with unrewarding grunt work when you need to.

1. Visualize your eventual success. Now imagine you have been asked to talk to an audience about how you achieved your goal, despite the odds. What inspiring advice would you share to motivate your audience to keep going, particularly when the going gets tedious?

2. Write down your words of wisdom and make a pact with yourself to live them on a half-hour-by-half-hour basis. As incentive, tell yourself you'll take a five-minute break at the end of every half-hour of work.

3. Just before you take a break, flash back on your visualization and see yourself delivering your advice to your audience. Don't be surprised to find yourself practising what you preach.

SIXTEEN

Yes, but I don't have the patience

I'm the most impatient person I've ever met. I like strong tea, but do I wait for the tea to steep four minutes in the pot? No, as soon as I pour in the boiling water, I pour myself a cup and whine about the weak, flavourless brew. In one of my many attempts to find a meditative practice I could stick with, I took up ikebana, the art of flower arranging. Apparently, it's not okay to bunch as many flowers as you can in your fist and try to cut off all the ends in one fell swoop. The teacher suggested I try pottery. The pottery teacher suggested I try tranquilizers. I have to admit, I tend to seek instant gratification. Sadly, I learned the hard way that follow-through will truly test the impatient.

That's a dilemma, because not everyone with an ambition is content to wait for her efforts to pay off. Some of us would rather cut our losses and move on than hang around, hoping something will happen before the next ice age. Gurus of all stripes are forever droning on and on that patience is a

215

virtue. I'm sure if I could make it through an entire lecture on the subject, I'd have to agree. But I do think there's something to be said for us fast-talking toe-tappers. We get things done, on the double.

Speaking for myself, I recognize that I'm not the most meticulous of workers, but if I decide to paint a room, it's finished in a day. Sure, there are a few paint splotches on the furniture, windowsills, and floor – the ultra-finicky might point out that there are more than a few – but most important, the job is over and done with.

When you're used to living life in the fast lane, it's hard to stick with a project that fails to move at a nice speedy clip. But, say the gurus with fingers wagging, Rome wasn't built in a day, a good wine takes years to mature, and no one can learn Spanish overnight. Their point, apparently, is that if everyone demanded instant results, the world would be deprived of the Roman Coliseum, you'd never enjoy a decent Cabernet, and few would speak Spanish as a second language.

How to endure when endurance goes against the grain

Patience is defined in the dictionary as the ability to endure waiting or delay without becoming annoyed or upset, or to persevere calmly when faced with difficulties. For the impatient, the key then is to figure out a way to endure when endurance goes against the grain. Luckily, people with the follow-through factor have strategies to offer.

It took Jacky five long years to get her idea for a parenting show on the air at her radio network. She was working as a news writer at the station when she wrote up the proposal. Barry, the program director, told her to put together a demo – a sample show. After she submitted her demo, Barry told her he'd "think about it." Intermittently, she would check in with Barry and send him emails, each one showing new facts and figures about why the parenting show would be of interest to listeners. After years of hearing "We'll see," she had an impromptu meeting with the head of sales while they were both waiting for the elevator. He told her they'd need a heavyweight sponsor for the program and suggested she talk to one of the sales reps about it. She put together a new proposal, made a new demo, and eventually got to produce a ninety-second parenting item a day, as well as a radio column on Saturday mornings.

Jacky, by her own admission, lacks forbearance. She's the reason why retailers need cashiers on speed. Jacky thinks nothing of spending four hours in a boutique monopolizing the fitting room, but if, heaven forbid, she has to wait in line at the cash, she'll drop her collection of hard-earned finds on the nearest surface and rush out as if her house were on fire.

So how did Jacky manage to keep pushing her idea for five unrewarding years and not just rip up her proposal and forget about it? She bought a new daybook every year, and when she sat down in January to write in annual appointments and school holidays, she made sure she also inscribed the word "parenting" on the first Wednesday of February, May, August, and November. When she hit one of those Wednesdays, she would write: "Find latest stats on moms in our target market. Find latest info about popularity of parenting shows. Find one fun parenting fact. Email program director."

Jacky kept moving the project between the back burner and the front burner. Each time she brought it forward, she identified a few small, easy steps she could take to try and make the show happen. And every time she completed those steps, she felt she had accomplished something. It's the difference between standing at the bus stop for ages and deciding to walk from one stop to the next. In both cases, you're still waiting for the Number 29, but it's more gratifying to speed walk from street corner to street corner than it is to stand tensely glaring into the distance.

As Jacky so poetically put it, "Waiting sucks." The reason it sucks is because when you're in wait mode, you have no control. When you're standing in a long line at the Gap on Boxing Day, you can't storm the counter, shove the cashier aside, and start ringing in your half-price sweaters. When you need to book a flight to Prague with a stopover in Amsterdam, you can scream into the phone all you want, but that's not going to get an airline rep to deliver you from the recorded "please hold" message any faster. You can't make time fly. And you can't force decision-makers to give you a response by a certain day (for which you still have to wait) if they aren't prepared to do so.

The only thing you can do is dig deep to determine the few elements that are in your control and focus on those. In Jacky's case, she put together a schedule for sending fact-filled emails to prod her program director. Here's another reality bite. Jacky doesn't actually credit those emails, at least not directly, for getting her what she wanted. The way she sees it, if she hadn't bumped into the sales manager, she could still be emailing the program director. And he'd still be hitting the Delete button and avoiding her in the halls. But she does admit that if she had given up on her idea after her first attempt, she wouldn't have pitched the sales manager at the elevator, and certainly wouldn't be producing mini–parenting shows today.

Let's rewind the tape and see what might have happened if Jacky had bumped into the sales manager four years after she had given up on her idea. Here's how their conversation might have gone:

"I had an idea once for a parenting show," Jacky says.

"Not our thing. We target women at work," says Sales Manager.

"I know that, but a lot of the women in our demographic have kids."

"Yeah, but we're the 'at work' station, not the 'at home' one. So how's life in the newsroom?"

"Fine. But I tell you, the parenting show I envisioned would have really connected with our audience. I don't know why Barry didn't go for it."

Elevator arrives.

219

"Like I said, Jacky, it's not our thing. What floor do you want?"

Now here's how the actual conversation went:

"Did Barry mention I have a great idea for a parenting show?"

"Not our thing. We target women at work."

"I know that, but a lot of women in our demographic have kids."

"Yeah, but we're the 'at work' station, not the 'at home' one . . ."

"Are you kidding me? I just saw a survey that showed ninety percent of women think about their kids a minimum of five times during the day. And you know what they're thinking about? They're thinking about whether they'll have another battle over homework that night, or if their kid really is an outcast because she's not wearing cool clothes. I tell you, people would schedule their coffee break around this show because it speaks to what's eating away at them. I just emailed Barry some stats that show parenting magazines are growing in leaps and bounds. Parenting info is huge; parents are nervous wrecks – they want help."

"Well, a daytime talk show is not our format. But maybe we could run some sponsored mini-features. Talk to Norma about that and see what you can put together to interest a client."

Elevator arrives.

"What do you mean by a mini-feature?"

"Something like 'A parenting minute brought to you by Fresh Fruit Bars.'"

"Okay, well, a minute is pretty short, but you know, we could do something like that to start . . ."

Jacky could not have had the conversation she did if she hadn't kept researching and promoting her project. What's more, she said that if after years of not thinking about the parenting show at all, the sales manager had suggested she produce a tip of the day for parents, she probably wouldn't have been open to the idea. It wasn't what she had envisioned at the start and she wouldn't have felt committed, or still eager enough, to be flexible. But after years of actively trying to get a show on the air, she just wanted to do *something*. And it worked out well. She loves doing the tips, and the work led her to develop a niche as a parenting writer.

Impatience breeds doubt

Impatient people have a bad habit of thinking of time as pages flying off a calendar in fast motion. They throw around the ominous warning that if things don't happen quickly, "It'll be *too late*." They don't ask themselves what exactly it will be "too late" for. It's not as if they're counting down until doomsday as they drum their fingers on the table. No, behind the urgency is fear, not a fear of the world imploding before they get a chance to accomplish their objective, but a fear of disappointment. They don't trust that whatever they want to happen will happen.

They fret that someone with the same idea will get to the finish line first, that people will forget about them, that some unforeseen circumstance will force them off their path. They want to accomplish their goals *right now,* otherwise they're not sure they'll ever get accomplished. If someone could just give them a guarantee, they might relax a little.

People with the follow-through factor insist that the only guarantee possible is the one you give yourself.

A client writing her first mystery, which has bottled drinking water as its theme and a water sommelier as the amateur detective, was frantic that an established author would come up with the same notion and get a book out first. With her heart in her throat, Barb spent time every Saturday scouring new mystery releases to see if one had delved into the cutthroat world of designer waters. If her concern had been spurring her on to write day and night, it wouldn't have been a problem. But instead, her impatience to get the novel finished and in the mail to agents was giving her a serious case of writer's block. Barb needed to allow herself time to try out different plots and characters, but she didn't feel she could spare the time to experiment.

I had two words for Barb: "So what?" So what if another author comes out with a story that has a similar theme? As an English literature professor told me decades ago, "There are no new ideas, only fresh approaches." We live in a copycat culture. The minute an original new product, service, technique, book, or movie appears there are a dozen imitations right

behind it. In an age where just about every idea can be repli-
cated in the blink of an eye, you win if you do it best, not
necessarily if you do it first.

Impatient people typically think of their project as an air-
plane flight they can't afford to miss. And what happens
when you do get into a traffic jam on the way to the airport
and your non-refundable charter flight leaves without you?
You curse, you feel miserable and angry with yourself and
the world, you go home, and you go to bed. End of trip.

People with the follow-through factor think of their project
not as the flight, but as the destination city itself. They may
miss a few flights to Paris, they may have to make some
unforeseen stops, but they know that one way or another,
they'll get there.

NOTE TO SELF: For those among us who gun our engines at red lights, setting goals that can take time to materialize demands a more serene approach to life than may be comfortable. If you're restless, ask yourself, "Why do I have to get an answer, or a result, this week?" Nine times out of ten, you'll answer irritably, "Because I need it to move to the next step." But chances are there is something else, even a small thing, you could do to advance your goal in the meantime. You'll argue that while there might be some little steps you could take, without the key piece you won't meet your deadline. So consider changing your deadline. If you set the date, you can move it if you want. Deadlines are great motivators for keeping up momentum, but you don't need to make every deadline a now-or-never, do-or-die proposition. Of course, if you are up against a timeline that must be met, then you have no choice but to insist that people give you the answer or input you need by a certain date. But if you're working with a self-imposed deadline that is proving to be unrealistic for you, you may be setting yourself up for failure if you're not flexible.

"Patience is also a form of action"

Jason, a Ferrari salesman, had to learn patience on the job or get into another line of work. He takes inspiration from the French sculptor Auguste Rodin, who said, "Patience is also a form of action." A Ferrari is not an impulse buy, not even for those who can afford $250,000 for a car. For Jason, almost every sale comes after a very long, slow dance with the customer, marked by extended periods of sitting around like a wallflower.

Like Jacky, Jason gives every interaction his best shot, and at regular predetermined intervals sends out customized, tantalizing info about the car to an interested customer. But in between, when the potential customer is out of sight, Jason puts him out of mind and concentrates on other things. He says if he didn't, he'd go berserk with the waiting, wondering, and wanting.

Jason stops himself from obsessing by choosing to believe the deal will come through, eventually. He keeps sane by defining *eventually* as "two to five years." Jason explains, "I relax because I'm convinced that I'll get a positive result, providing I do the best I can to build up relationships with potential buyers and sustain their interest. But I eliminate my impatience by telling myself that it's not going to happen tomorrow, or even next year."

Impatient people who manage to follow through warn that if they gave way to negative feelings, one of two things would happen. They would come off as pushy, even desperately aggressive, which would just turn people off, or they'd just give up in frustration. So, like Jason, those with the follow-through factor make a point of deliberately setting realistic deadlines for their projects, which allows them to concentrate on process rather than demanding instant results, of themselves and of others.

225

CUE CARD

- We get impatient when we can't make things happen when and how we want. It makes us crazy to not have control. The most effective way to counter impatience is to set up a series of achievable mini-steps that we have the power to accomplish.

- Ultimately, behind our sense of urgency is our fear that if we don't realize our ambition now, it may never happen, for a variety of reasons. There's no way to guarantee that the competition won't overtake you or that other unforeseen circumstances won't force you to detour. It is possible that between here and getting there, you may have to rethink your approach somewhat, but so long as you continue to follow through, you can be sure you will realize your intentions.

- Put your focus on process, not on deadlines, and you'll discover you're actually more patient than you could ever have imagined. And repeatedly remind yourself of the famous quote "Patience is also a form of action."

Designing a deadline that works for you

A deadline is a useful whip-cracking tool to move us to action. It forces a sense of urgency that motivates us to stop procrastinating and start racing against time. But a deadline is only helpful if it's realistic. An unworkable deadline is like an unsolvable math problem. After our initial first attempt, we resign ourselves to the fact that our efforts are hopeless, and give up.

One of my clients was a discontented senior executive who had grown bored of working in banking. A few years earlier, he'd attempted to find a job in an entirely different sector. He'd engaged a professional resumé-writing service and given himself four months to find a high-level position in a new industry. When he didn't have a job offer by the time he hit his self-imposed deadline, he told himself he was never going to get one. I suggested we work on an eighteen-month transition plan. Both his attitude, and his results, dramatically improved.

Make a deadline for yourself, but don't let impatience prompt you to pick a date out of the air. Those with the follow-through factor know that the only good deadline is a feasible one. Answer the following questions to make sure your deadline is a fair deal to make with yourself.

227

1. What's your deadline?

_____

_____

2. What needs to happen for you to make this deadline?

_____

_____

3. What is in your control to make happen?

_____

_____

4. What could cause hold-ups that are beyond your control?

_____

_____

5. What can you do to keep moving forward on your path while waiting?

_____

_____

6. Review your answers to the above questions. Is the deadline you set for yourself realistic?

_____

_____

SEVENTEEN

Yes, but what if I fail?

I s it really true that it's better to have loved and lost than never to have loved at all? The answer depends on when you're doing the asking. At the time of a break-up, you'd have to say no, it's not true at all. Given your druthers, you'd take a pass on spending long days and nights camped on the couch, wiping your tears off the TV remote, eating nothing but tortilla chips. But ask that question ten years after the fact, during a weekend getaway with old pals, and you'll open a bottle of wine and relive the best and worst of times with great relish. Of course, it's always possible that the old wound still stings, but at least you'll have a dramatic story to share.

The same principle applies to the question, is it better to have acted and lost than never to have acted at all? In his book *Stumbling on Happiness,* Daniel Gilbert has compiled the research that proves we would rather take our chances than play it safe. He concludes that over time people of every age and walk of life feel more regret about what they didn't do than what they did. This is partly because it's easier to justify failure to ourselves than is it to explain why we wimped out and didn't do anything. We applaud ourselves and others for trying, even when things don't work out as hoped. "I tried my best" is a badge of honour. "I didn't try" is a blight on our character.

Roger is a perfect example. He ran a gourmet shop that was doing fine, but too quickly opened a second one in another location that went bust. He lost his shirt. During the period when he was sinking deeper and deeper into debt, if you'd have asked if he regretted his bold action, he would have thrown a jar of killer chili peppers at your head. But time makes great revisionists of us all. Today he'll tell you that he learned an enormous amount from that experience and is a far better businessman as a result. In fact, he's now working as a franchise consultant.

"What would life be like if you hadn't tried to expand?" I asked him.

"I've asked myself that question many times," he said. "My sense is that I'd be sitting in my original shop feeling like I could, I should be doing more. I think I'd feel frustrated and disappointed with myself."

Inaction may be safe, but as the years go by, it starts to feel and sound a lot like cowardice. Fear of failure is propelled by concern that the steps we take may land us in a worse situation than the one we're in right now. You worry that if you invest time, money, energy, and reputation into an idea that goes wrong, you won't just be back at square one, you may be in emotional, and possibly financial, deficit.

You've got a great reputation at work. Are you going to jeopardize it by suggesting that you crack open a new, non-traditional market? What if you don't end up doing well in this area? You won't be the success story around the office anymore. Then again, every office star has to find new ways to keep shining or be obliterated by up-and-coming hotshots. Still, go out on a limb, and the branch could fall under your weight. Is it worth it? Yes, it's worth it. For no other reason than failure and inaction both lead to the same pit stop – regret. But at least with failure, you can boast about your efforts, you can figure that you learned something, and you can leave the pit stop stronger and move down the road. If you don't follow through on ideas, you just keep playing with your worry beads. First you mull over how great things could have been. Then you mull over what terrible things might have happened. Then you return to thinking how great things could have been . . . ad nauseum.

How to find some wisdom in the ruins

Of course, it's one thing to say we learn from our failures and it's another to actually be able to find wisdom among the ruins. Those with the follow-through factor become adept at this particular talent. After all, getting from here to there is hardly like stepping into an elevator and pressing the penthouse button. It's more of a two-steps-forward, one-step-backward progression at the best of times.

In listening to those who follow through detail how they overcame various fiascos, it's clear that the secret to picking yourself up and dusting yourself off is to see yourself as separate from your failure. In other words, those who trip along the way to somewhere stop and assess why they didn't see the pothole on their path, but at no time do they consider themselves to be stumbling, hopeless klutzes.

To learn from failure, you can't take it personally. People who follow through typically attribute failure to a lack of information, an honest miscalculation, or events outside their control. They hold themselves accountable, but they don't blame themselves. There's a big distinction between the two. To hold yourself accountable is to recognize that you have the power to make choices and the strength to be responsible for them. Working from a perspective of power, you're willing to revisit a disappointing situation and ask yourself what you could have done differently. To blame yourself is to hit yourself on the head with your hairbrush every morning while repeating into the mirror, "I'm useless." Since those with the follow-through factor don't see failure as a personal flaw, they don't use their hairbrush as a hammer.

232   A sought-after figure skating coach shared how she chooses among the many skaters who want to train with her: "I don't care about how many times people fall," she said. "I care about how many times they get up. I can only

work with people who know they are not their mistakes; those are the people who truly believe they can improve."

Of course, rare is the person who can go straight from disaster to cool contemplation without a bit of ranting and raving at the gods. But once you get that out of your system, those with follow-through say the next step is to brew some coffee, relax, and look at your situation as if it's a crossword puzzle in the Saturday newspaper. Stay detached while studying the clues that forewarned a collapse. The goal is to figure out why things went wrong so you can fix the problem, figure out how to work around it, or, if necessary, accept it.

Why did I fail? vs. What could I have done differently?

When Roger reviewed his situation, he didn't ask himself, "Why did I fail?" Instead, he asked the question that all those with the follow-through factor ask themselves when they hit a bump in the road: "What could I have done differently?"

The problem with asking yourself "Why did I fail?" is that you're setting yourself up to be judged by the nastiest critic of all – yourself. The question carries inherent blame and is a direct path to the hairbrush bop. "I failed because I have a doorknob for a brain. I'm a moron." This is not the kind of uplifting thinking that gets you back on the road as a stronger, wiser person. It's also not the kind of thinking that will free you to follow through. As mentioned earlier, follow-through requires an adventurous spirit. And, in turn, an adventurous spirit requires a willingness to allow ourselves a few wrong turns as we explore new territory. There's not a businessperson, scientist, artist, or athlete in the world who hasn't made some errors in judgment on their way to success. As Oscar Wilde put it, "Experience is simply the name we give our mistakes."

On the other hand, asking yourself what you could have done differently softens the self-flagellation and moves you quickly to learning, fixing, accepting. Roger said he could have done more analysis of his finances, and the marketplace, before deciding to open a second store. His decision-making was uninformed because he didn't have a lot of data. That learning has helped him become a wise business consultant.

Even when we recognize that we learn best from mistakes, we remain paralyzed by fear of failure. Failure is a lot like ripping off a Band-Aid: we anticipate it's going to hurt a lot more than it actually does. Simply put, there is some pain, we do get upset, but we get over it. There are hundreds of studies that show that negative outcomes don't impact us for as long, or as intensely, as we expect.

Yet we spend every day convincing ourselves we'll be immeasurably affected by whatever positive or negative events may happen in our future. We anticipate that a promotion, a house on the beach, a fridge with a built-in cocktail shaker will bring us boundless joy. At the same time, we imagine we'll die if we lose our jobs, get dumped, or go bankrupt. You'd think we'd all know from our personal history that while we experience blips of happiness and depression, we end up taking the good and the bad in stride, and coping. But instead, we continue to predict that situations will overturn our world as we know it. In fact, reality is usually far less extreme than our stories about it. Our storytelling may be rife with dramatic flourishes that we toss in like chili flakes, but our actual day-to-day life is significantly milder than we make it out to be.

Nancy's resumé reads like an obit column. She has worked at so many magazines and specialty newspapers that have gone under that people wonder if she's a jinx. But while publishers might want to dive for cover when they see her coming, Nancy isn't bothered by the trail of bankrupt businesses she leaves in her wake. She doesn't worry about what she'll do or feel when she finds herself out of work yet again. "Been there, done that so many times," she laughed. "I know how the process works. First, you feel like, 'Oh God, I don't know what I'm going to do.' Then you move to, 'Okay, I gotta get a grip,' and finally you arrive at, 'That's life. Now I need to figure out what action to take.'"

"The first time I lost my job, I was frantic about my future," Nancy recalled. "I took the first job I could find. It was with a junky fashion newspaper that was really more like an advertising flyer. That paper lasted all of five minutes. Then I went to a new city magazine, which died the year after I arrived. Next was a free entertainment weekly that crashed and burned in about eight months. And that's not the end of it. But as a result of this, I have such a strong

235

sense of my own ability to survive. You're up, you're down, and eventually you're up again." Today, Nancy is a rare breed of freelancer who doesn't panic when work is sparse but sends out story pitches in the mornings and goes to movies in the afternoons.

Failure sounds worse than it is

Those with the follow-through factor know from experience that failing isn't quite as traumatic as people imagine it will be. There are so few situations in life that can't be handled, although the solution you eventually come up with may be different from what you could have predicted. But you can always rely on the guarantee that follow-through offers: you don't always know where exactly your perseverance will take you, but you know it'll get you somewhere.

Then again, if you're madly in love with a particular dream, you may not want to take any chances at all with it. If that's your dilemma, then your fear of failure has you pinned in an iron headlock.

A dream can be so rewarding. We feel great as we describe in detail how our future will unfold. It's like a lottery ticket. From the time we buy the ticket to the day of the draw, we get to have so much fun fantasizing about the cute little chalet in Aspen that we'll buy with our winnings.

Laura tells everyone she's a writer. It's her identity badge. Her job at the bank is just a way to pay the bills while she crafts her hen-humour novel about a mom who hits menopause at the same time as her daughter hits puberty. She's recounted the general gist of the novel and the same two scenes to so many people, so many times, that she admits she feels as if she's already written the book. She hasn't.

Laura has written and rewritten about twenty-five pages over the past four years. I wouldn't bet the house that she'll actually get beyond that, because the longer Laura talks about her project, the more obvious it becomes that she likes the idea of being a writer much more than writing. She wants her name on the cover of a best-seller that will be made into a movie starring Susan Sarandon and Miley Cyrus. As long as she keeps talking about it, the project is real enough to make her feel as if she's an actual author, with every chance at fame and fortune. But if she writes the book and sends it out to agents and no one likes it, she figures she's not just getting rejected, she's getting cut off from her dream.

I alluded to Laura's situation when talking to a client who has almost finished her first book. Does she have the same fear? "Not at all," she said. "My definition of a writer is someone who writes. I may not be a published author for quite some time, if ever, but so long as I'm sitting at my computer writing books, I think of myself a writer. Why wouldn't I?"

Mason is more like Laura. He's a recruiter who has been talking about producing a series of videocasts for job-hunters for his company for about two years. Together, we broke down the project into all of its components and wrote out a micro-step action plan. Mason's employer likes the

237

idea but isn't pressuring him to follow through, and Mason certainly hasn't been. Why not? Mason has grandiose ideas that he doesn't want to reel in. When challenged, he admits he enjoys conceiving and talking about potentially award-winning shorts. But he wants to go from idea straight to standing on a podium accepting his trophy. If he can't be sure that his work will result in industry recognition of his talent, he'd rather just stay in dream mode.

Dreams can turn into bugaboos

Over time, a dream that never takes shape in any way becomes a bugaboo. At some point, it will hang over your head as a failure. Ironically, the very failure you fear is virtually guaranteed, not because you took steps and made blunders along the way, but because you didn't do anything. That's why everyone who follows through shares the same mindset when it comes to dreams. They refuse to get caught up in fantasies about happily-ever-after fairy-tale endings. Instead, they stay focused on the very real day-to-day process required to achieve their goals.

Fear of failure may also be triggered by a surprising source – our very own support team. Since we trust that our nearest and dearest have only our best interests at heart, we pay attention when they predict that nothing good will come of our straying into new territory. We become anxious as we listen to their doom-and-gloom warnings. And amid their hand-wringing, and ours, we forget to grill them on when and how they acquired their psychic power to foretell our future.

Voula's story illustrates the point. Voula's family owned an accounting firm, and from the time she brought home her first A in math, she was expected to join the company as an accountant or corporate lawyer. On January 1, 2000, the usually acquiescent Voula caused shockwaves around the dinner table when she announced she would like to quit filing taxes for the corporation and instead go to community college and study food and hospitality.

"My father said, 'We are a family of business professionals, not cooks.' My mother said, 'You're mad; the hours are terrible, and you get treated like dirt in a kitchen.' My older brother said, 'You're too old; you'll never get a job.' My brother-in-law said, 'There's no money in it. How are you going to keep your condo?' My sister said, 'It's hot and greasy in a kitchen. Your hair will go frizzy and your skin will break out.'" When Voula argued to family and friends that she had always wanted to be a chef, they all said she was more than welcome to cook dinner for them anytime.

Voula had to agree that everyone made sense. That year, she kept her job and bought a lot of cookbooks. But one day she was sitting in a meeting, bored as usual, when she became acutely aware that everyone around the table was nodding his head in disconcerting unison at everything her father was saying. The old cliché that people are like sheep came galloping to mind. Then and there, she said

239

she realized that we all want each other to think as we do and do as we do. There's safety and community in being of one mind.

One of the most valuable pieces of advice I ever received came from a newspaper editor who told me the "secret to everything" was to examine the original source of any piece of information or point of view. "Look to the source, and all will be made clear to you," he intoned from behind his desk. When Voula looked at the source of the insistent advice she was receiving, she discovered something that made a huge impact on her decision-making process. The people in her life didn't care about what she wanted to do; they cared about what she *didn't* want to do. She didn't want to follow in their footsteps.

When she scratched the surface, Voula learned her father had, once upon a time, thought of becoming a tennis pro, but dismissed his ambition for what he considered to be a more career-smart move. He had made a financially rewarding, sensible sacrifice, and so should Voula. Her brother didn't mind his job, but his greatest personal satisfaction came from his basement recording studio. If having an after-hours interest was good enough for him, why wasn't it good enough for Voula? Not one of Voula's personal advisers had ever worked in a kitchen, or wanted to. They weren't offering informed opinions; they were urging Voula to heed their own choices, beliefs, and fears. Voula is now a full-time student at a culinary arts school.

YES, BUT WHAT IF I FAIL?

NOTE TO SELF: Always get to the source of people's fears for you. When someone is telling you all the terrible things that will likely happen if you pursue your plan, don't beat around the bush but ask straight up, and even a mite aggressively if necessary, "How do you know?" You'll likely discover that their information is sketchy at best. Mostly, people will quote a friend of a friend or say they read it somewhere. If appropriate, look at them as if they've just told you that the moon is made of Brie, shake your head, and say, "Why would I let one article or the alleged experience of one person, whom I don't even know, influence my life?" If you need to take a more diplomatic tack, you can always go with, "I'll research that point some more and get back to you." Don't neglect to put heavy emphasis on the word research. If they have first-hand experience, learn what you can from it, then move on to ask this question: "Isn't it possible that somewhere out there, some people have managed to succeed?" They'll say, "Yes, but . . ." Talk over the "but" and say, "I rest my case." As religious writer Edwin Cole advised, "Don't let someone else create your world for you, for when they do, they will always make it too small."

Make sure you're wrestling with *your* fear, not someone else's

We all have enough fears of our own. We don't need to take on anyone else's fears for us, no matter how seemingly well-intentioned they are. If we're going to wrestle with fear, the least we can do is make sure it's our own we're trying to subdue. Following through involves change, and change is always threatening to someone. Like the unhappily married couple who counsel you against ending your own miserable relationship, people who are willing to shake things up and risk failure make others nervous.

Those with the follow-through factor recognize that some failure is inevitable along the way. They define failures as setbacks, not as personal inadequacy. To the contrary, all the successful people I interviewed clearly liked themselves for going after their goals, even though at times they all were frustrated, and sometimes felled, by uninformed decisions they made or circumstances beyond their control. They could tolerate letdowns and obstacles. What they couldn't tolerate was inaction.

CUE CARD

- If you suffer from a paralyzing case of fear of failure, remember that it's far easier to justify and accept mistakes than it is to explain inaction, even to ourselves.
- Failure doesn't hurt nearly as much as we think it will. We always exaggerate how we'll feel in the future.
- It's true that when you take action, you don't have a guarantee that your dream will have a fairy-tale ending. But at least you will have a real story to tell, good or bad, which brings more meaning and momentum to your life than a goal never pursued.

EXERCISE
Letters from the future

All of us have thought back to the forks along our road and wondered what would have happened if we had chosen another course of action. Today, you stand at yet another fork in your road. Are you going to follow through on your idea, or are you not?

To help you decide, fast-forward to your birthday five years from now by filling in the blanks in these two letters, crafted to give you a sneak preview of how you might feel years from now if you do, and if you don't, travel the road of your ambition.

I followed through:

Dear _____ ,

 I can't believe it has been five years since I first wrote you about my plan to _____

_____ ,
I remember wondering back then if I would actually make it happen. Well, I did.

 I can still recall ticking off all the reasons why I shouldn't proceed. I was too _____

_____

_____ .

I don't think there was an excuse I didn't try to buy for myself. But then came the turning point.

243

I realized that in five years, I would be turning _____ years old. (Funny how it doesn't sound as old to me now as it did then.) I thought, I can hit that birthday feeling great that I

_____

_____

_____ or I can hit that birthday with regret that I_____

_____

_____

_____.

So right then and there, I decided I would take the first micro-step towards it, and I'd keep taking one micro-step after another, uphill, downhill, through some muddy patches, until I reached my goal. What kept me going was faith that I was doing the right thing because_____

_____

_____

_____.

Today, I'm pleased that _____

_____

_____.

Some of the things that I do now that give me a real boost are

_____

_____

_____

_____.

When people meet me, they always want to know about

_____

_____

_____

What else has changed in my life? For one thing, I'm not the same person I was five years ago. There's been a change in my relationship with myself. I'm less _____ and more _____. And my relationships with _____ have changed too, because I _____

_____

_____

_____

_____

Five years ago, I promised myself I'd be toasting myself on this birthday, and so I will. Here's to me, for _____

_____

_____

_____

_____

_____

_____

And here's to the future, with all my best.
Yours,

I didn't follow through:

Dear _____,

    Remember five years ago, when I had that big idea to
_____
_____
_____.

I still say that it was a brilliant idea. But I never made it happen. Looking back, I suppose I was too _____
_____
_____ and _____
_____
_____ to stick with it. Do I
have regrets? Every now and then, I catch myself wondering
_____
_____
_____
_____.

    I suppose I thought things would just happen over time,
naturally, without me having to _____
_____
_____
so that by now I'd _____

_____
_____
_____.

It's a funny thing about time; the years can fly by, but you can find that you haven't moved much. If I could do over the last five years, I would _____

_____

_____

_____

_____

_____.

    I'm still doing _____

_____.

And I'm still feeling _____

and _____.

    I'm still hoping and waiting for _____

_____.

_____

_____ just as I was five years earlier.

    So what have I learned? Well, I learned _____

_____

_____

_____

_____

_____

_____.

    Regards,

I have a confession to make. This book took me years to write, and many times I came within inches of adding the half-written manuscript to a stack of incomplete ones that are sitting in a box. I came close to being defeated by every single "but" I discuss in these chapters. I did question my passion. When a literary agent suggested that I use my research to write a novel instead of this book, I spent months waffling. I did wonder if this endeavour was the best use of my time. I did loose energy. I initially self-published this book without having a clue how to go about it. I did question the money it required. I was impatient with myself and the process. I did walk the aisles of bookstores and wonder if I should bother. Did I experience doubt and self-criticism? Need you ask?

As I said in the opening pages, my mother lacked the follow-through factor, and this acorn didn't fall far from the tree. This book isn't just a compilation of tried-and-true strategies that have worked for clients, it's also my personal journey. While that might seem odd given my years of experience with helping people attain their goals, we all know too well that it's hard to do for yourself what you do for others. I take my place in line behind managers who give everyone but themselves a break, behind accountants who delay filing their own taxes, and behind a famous hypnotherapist with insomnia. After he told me that, no, he wasn't joking, I tried to smooth ruffled feathers by admitting that I'm a follow-through expert with an unfinished mystery, a half-written memoir, and a handful of grant applications in a drawer. And no, I'm not joking.

So the fact that you are reading this book is the strongest proof I can offer that if you follow the thinking and strategies in these chapters, you will definitely get to where you want to go. For each person, the process will unfold differently. For my part, I didn't always instantly apply the wisdom of those with the follow-through factor to my own situation. But like bits of a song that get into your head, their words to live by stuck in my mind.

When life became crazy busy and I didn't have a drop of energy to spare for this project, the notion of doing just one micro-task niggled at me. Eventually, I gave in and made a pact with myself to jot down a thought a day in a notebook. When I became impatient with how long this project was taking, recalling that I didn't have a plane to catch stopped me from deleting the file in moments of

249

restless impetuosity. I turned my battle cry of "Not this time" into a morning chant to help me break the old habit of jumping ship before completing a journey. My "letter from the future" became my manifesto. I stuck it in a frame, deliberately putting it on top of a silhouette picture of me reading in a hammock under palm trees. I had to stop reminding myself that I'd rather be reading instead of staring at a blank computer screen, trying to think of a way to open a new chapter.

From my own struggles I know that if, at the very minimum, you do nothing but keep these follow-through factor strategies in your back pocket, you'll eventually achieve your breakthroughs. When I think back on my rocky progression, I am reminded of an incident from my early twenties. At the time, I owned an old, temperamental television set that would turn on only when you hit it in a certain spot. One whack didn't always work; sometimes you had to hit it repeatedly. I kept a shoe by the TV for that purpose. I passed that shoe to a guy-friend who had dropped by one day to watch a show. He tossed it over his shoulder. Then he spent forty minutes fiddling with the set. Eventually he sat back and stared at the black screen while I continued to examine the ceiling tiles. Moments before his show was over, he picked up the shoe. If I had known then that I'd too resist strategies that were proven to work, I wouldn't have been so smug. In any event, the point is that once you know about the shoe, you're going to use it sooner or later.

The one motivator you can count on is that success inspires success. Push beyond one obstacle, and you'll push beyond another. Follow through on one plan, and you'll follow through on another. I used to marvel at how quickly my clients would move from completing one goal to starting on the next. Now I understand first-hand that once you've flexed your follow-through factor, there's no turning back. You're not the same person you were at the start of a project. That's because follow-through is a state of mind.

Once you make a deal with yourself to do what's right by you, it's downright impossible to ever again think that you're at the mercy of others to make your ambitions happen. You no longer believe in killing time while hoping for money or contacts to drop from the sky or how-to manuals to land in your mailbox. You know the time and circumstances are never ideal, but having experienced the adventurous follow-through state of mind once, you transform into an explorer. You accept that you're bound to come up against situations that you couldn't have predicted, but you don't sweat it because you know that you can figure out a way to get around just about anything.

I didn't move as quickly as I might have to complete this book, but the little kick that I give myself for that is nothing compared to the enormous pat on the back that I give myself for getting it done. I'm really pleased with myself. And that's what it all comes down to. This endeavour strengthened my relationship with myself; I feel I have done something right by me.

Throughout the process, I kept reviewing my motivation for pursuing my ambition, and I urge you to also continually check in with yourself. In my case, I wanted to share the indisputable evidence I had gathered that the follow-through factor works: it's doable, it delivers results, and when you implement the strategies for persevering in the face of doubts and demands, you feel great about yourself. Communicating this knowledge was the best way I could think of to support people in their goals. And being supportive in a pragmatic way makes me feel good. So that's why I had faith that this was the right project for me. And what starts in faith ends in fulfillment.

I know that each one of you reading this can follow through to make your idea happen. Just flipping through these pages is the first micro-step in crossing the bayou that lies between your ambition and your achievement of it. Carry this book as you would a map, and keep walking forward. Micro-step by micro-step, you'll find yourself on one of the most defining, and rewarding, journeys of your life, and you'll have stories to show for it. When you reach your goal, you'll join the ranks of all those who have conquered every "but" and will never let another one stop them from going where they long to go. You'll become one of those people who have the follow-through factor. In other words, you'll be in control of your destiny.

Words to live by

If you remember nothing else, remember this about . . .

Follow-through: The worst thing that happens to those who fall short in follow-through is nothing. The opposite of success isn't failure, it's status quo. (Chapter 1)

Faith in yourself: Faith is about the relationship you have with yourself. You need to trust that pursuing your goal is worthy and the right thing for you to do, if for no other reason than you'll like yourself better for trying. (Chapter 2)

Knowing whether to pursue a goal: Understanding how activities link to your interests and values is the surest path to understanding the source of your faith. (Chapter 3)

Truth: Truth is defined as valid perspective. And every perspective has some validity. To help you figure out what's true for you, redefine truth as a source of positive energy. (Chapter 4)

Pointlessness: Nothing has meaning but the meaning you give it. If it's worthwhile to you, that's the whole point of going for it. (Chapter 5)

Choice: There's "good" and "not so good" on every road. It doesn't matter which path you pick; just pick one and start moving. (Chapter 6)

Passion: No one feels the love 24/7 when developing an idea and struggling to make it work. But when you stick with something, your affection for it grows, not diminishes. (Chapter 7)

Not having a clue: At some point you have to proceed, even though you lack experience. At that time, "fake it until you make it." (Chapter 8)

Being fearful: When fear and doubt are taunting you, get angry. Shout down your inner scaremongers with a verbal equivalent of a black-belt karate punch. When you get irritated and angry with fear, it turns from a snarling dog to one with its tail between its legs. (Chapter 9)

Time: Take stock of what you're saying "yes" to, and "no" to, throughout your day. If you don't think you have a moment to spare, remember that what you do with each moment is a matter of choice. (Chapter 10)

Energy: Ask yourself only once if you want to follow through. And when you come up with an answer, stick to it. Don't keep asking yourself the same question over and over again. You made your decision; now take the next micro-step. Even the smallest action unleashes energy. (Chapter 11)

Money: Give yourself permission to invest in your potential. Know that even if the worst happens and you don't get the payback you want, you'll survive and you'll have learned something you can apply to your future. (Chapter 12)

Intuition: You need to connect with your intuition to trust in yourself and project the message that you're confident and in control. To gain clarity in interactions with others, get out of your head and into theirs by asking questions about what they are thinking, needing, and feeling. (Chapter 13)

Lacking a mentor: Build your own mentor by patching together the compliments you've received, the wins you've had, and the fears – big and small – you've conquered over your lifetime. In the absence of a mentor, the mirror will have to do. (Chapter 14)

Boredom: Every project requires some grunt work, so be prepared to be bored, and don't run from it, because you won't be running towards anything; you'll only be running away from accomplishing your goal. Stick with boredom; more often than not it gives way to inspiration. (Chapter 15)

Impatience: We get impatient when we don't have the power to make things happen as we want, when we want. The way to counter impatience is to set up a series of achievable mini-steps that we have the power to accomplish. And remember, "Patience is also a form of action." (Chapter 16)

Failure: It's easier to accept and justify mistakes than it is to explain inaction, even to ourselves. (Chapter 17)

APPENDIX 2
Notes to self in a nutshell

Here are some quick comebacks and strategies for when you need them.

- If you build it, they still won't come, unless you go out and drag them to you. (Chapter 1)

- People may tell you they know you better than you know yourself. They don't. People may hold beliefs about what you ought to want or feel, but only you can know what truly excites or drains you. (Chapter 2)

- To those who would have you deliberate your options endlessly, there is only one thing to say: "The only bad choice is no choice." (Chapter 6)

- It's child's play to punch holes in an ambition and come up with a list of reasons why an idea is not worthy of pursuit. The only way to counterattack is to admit to the undeniable negative points and then follow up with equally undeniable positives. "You're right that most authors don't get rich off their books; they must get some other reward from writing." (Chapter 7)

- If you're already feeling uncertain, the last thing you need is to be confused by the uninformed opinions of friends, relatives, and colleagues who know even less than you about a particular subject. So if you're going to ask non-experts for direction, stick to extremely specific queries about one particular aspect of your project. (Chapter 8)

- Tell some people that you are going to take a chance, and they'll instantly try to engage you in the fear-mongering game: "What will you do if . . . any of these thousand disasters . . . should happen?" To bring this game to a quick stop, try saying, "I'll jump off that bridge when I get to it." (Chapter 9)

- Fatalists will tell you that if you don't revive an idea you've put on ice, it wasn't meant to be. That's just a story people sell to make you feel better about not following through on your ambition. You may have grown apart from your idea, but it doesn't mean that it wasn't a good one. (Chapter 10)

- Avoid telling people that you didn't fulfill your ambition because of their demands on your time. No one will take the rap for your frustration. Instead of an apology, you'll get a lecture on how you should have planned out your life better. (Chapter 10)

- We're as energetic as we think we are. And how we think is easily influenced by what we tell ourselves and what others say about us. Protect your energy by cutting short those who seem to delight in always telling you how tired, pale, exhausted, or stressed you look. To those who love to cluck that you look worn out, try this strategy. Say, "Don't worry, it's not just me. The lighting in here isn't flattering anyone." (Chapter 11)

- People understand when you fork out big bucks for a sports car or a wall-to-wall high-definition television, but tell them you're investing money in your ambition, and many times all you will hear is a skeptical "Good luck." No one relishes trading a tangible item or a cruise on the Mediterranean for a mere possibility of what might be. But ask yourself this: "Which choice could help me attain the future I want?" (Chapter 12)

- When asking yourself "what if?" don't let yourself, or anyone else, call your question stupid. Everything new started as a "silly" question. Likewise, don't allow "That would never work" as an answer. When you step outside reality and imagine the possibilities, you're stimulating your creativity. (Chapter 13)

- A weakness is not a curse that you're stuck with for life. People develop strength where they need to, when they want to. You might never become a world-class master in your area of challenge, but you certainly can improve dramatically. Even the biggest klutzes eventually manage to rollerblade to work without breaking any bones. (Chapter 14)

- There are many people out there who, being follow-through-challenged themselves, are eager to encourage you to take a break from pursuing your goal. Tell them you're bored and they'll show up at your door to rescue you. Do your future a favour. Don't open the door. (Chapter 15)

- Deadlines are great motivators for keeping up momentum, but you don't need to make every deadline a now-or-never, do-or-die proposition. If a deadline doesn't work for you, change it. You're only setting yourself up for failure if you're not flexible. (Chapter 16)

- Always get to the source of people's fears for you. When someone warns you of all the terrible things that will likely happen if you pursue your plan, ask straight up, and even a mite aggressively if necessary, "How do you know?" You'll typically discover their information is unreliable at best. Call them on it. As religious writer Edwin Cole advised, "Don't let someone else create your world for you, for when they do, they will always make it too small." (Chapter 17)

It's said that it takes a village to raise a child. It seems it also takes a village to get a book written.

First and foremost, many thanks to clients and others who have shared their stories with me. Don't worry, I've changed your names and details to safeguard confidentiality.

When I was writing humour columns for magazines, an editor once mentioned that she envied my ability to "effortlessly dash off " my essays. I gave a humble little shrug in response. But in my head I was screaming, "*Effortlessly* dash off?!!? You must be kidding." Those columns took hours of blood, sweat, and tears. Repeatedly throughout the night before a column was due, I would run upstairs to the bedroom, shake my husband awake, and ask in a tense voice, "Do you think this line is funny? . . . Oh really, you do? Then why aren't you laughing?" And I'd stomp back downstairs to try again.

Similarly, this book was not a one-draft effort. And I have many people to thank for feedback, encouragement, and patience while I wrote, deleted, wrote, and deleted again.

This book started as a self-published effort. Thanks to a terrific copy editor, Linda Jones, for her help on early drafts.

Leslie Hayden, an exceptionally creative strategist and very funny writer, helped me settle on a direction. I appreciate all those long-distance calls and emails, but would it be too much to ask to get together more often, maybe over champagne and scones at the Windsor Arms in Toronto?

I am grateful to Ann Jansen for her thorough review when the last thing in the world she had was the time – or the space. I'll never forget the picture of you sitting with my manuscript, a stack of highlighters, and pages of notes spread on a corner of a table while your entire house was in boxes around you. Never again will I sneak more than my fair share of a dessert from you.

Writing this book was an exercise in practising what I preach. I did build my own mentor, but I had invaluable help from Vivian George. Her encouragement and wisdom spurred me on.

For sounding boards, I could do no better than Lianne George, Robin King, Jacqueline Hayden, and Helen Dolik. Also, thanks to Karen Shopsowitz for her director's perspective and to Carl and Margaret Nygren for their support.

It's a sure thing that as you follow through on your ambition, you experience many highs. Thanks to Eric Jensen and Elizabeth Kribs at McClelland & Stewart for giving me one of my best dance-around-the-room moments.

And then there's my husband, Bill Nygren, a.k.a. "It's good." Through thick and thin, past doubt and into done, you've been the hand on my back and the arm around my shoulder. Thanks for always being my number-one fan.

Finally, thanks to Juliana for disputing the word "but" every time she hears it. And above all, to Mom, for making me determined to learn how to catch a dream or two.

No acknowledgments go to Toby and Olive. Your constant barking for cookies and attention really wasn't very helpful to the creative process. And I'm warning the two of you right now that next time I sit down to write a book, I'm hiding all your squeaky toys.